INCOMPATIBILITY:

Grounds for a GREAT MARRIAGE!

INCOMPATIBILITY:

Grounds for a GREAT MARRIAGE!

Chuck & Barb Snyder

QUESTAR PUBLISHERS, INC.

SISTERS, OREGON

INCOMPATIBILITY:
GROUNDS FOR A GREAT MARRIAGE!
© 1988 by Chuck & Barb Snyder
Published by Questar Publishers, Inc.

Eighth Printing, 1992

Printed in the United States of America

ISBN 0-945564-51-1

Cover design by Steve Diggs & Friends,
Nashville

Library of Congress Catalog Number: 88-18035

BARB:

To Chuck, my example.

To our children, who have grown up with us.

To Norma Smalley, Judy Burkett, Jack Arthur, and Sue Wright
who have ministered to us as much as their mates have.

And to the members of our Joint Heirs Class, who, for the last
nine years, have lived through our learning and teaching,
and helped us along our way.

CHUCK:

I would like to dedicate my portion of this book first of all to my
family—Barb, Tim, Tammie, Kjersten, Bev, Deb, Molly & Muffit—
who have put up with so much as I was learning the lessons of life.

Second, I want to express my deepest gratitude to the people who have
come alongside me to help make my marriage a thing of joy rather than
pain: Gary Smalley, Larry Burkett, Kay Arthur, and Larry Wright; and
to Norm and Bobbe Evans who introduced us to so many people who
have had a part in changing our lives.

CONTENTS

Finally—
a 50,000-Mile
Marriage!

IN THE EARLY DAYS of automobiles, when cars moved at a snail's pace, some models actually had steel tires. These cast-iron circles were meant to withstand whatever punishment the dirt roads of that time dished out. The tires actually outlasted many of the early cars they were placed on, but unfortunately, passengers in such vehicles had to endure an extremely bumpy ride.

As years went by and better engines dramatically increased traveling speeds, rubber tires were introduced. These provided a more cushioned ride that passengers loved. But at the higher speeds on the new asphalt roads, many of these rubber tires seemed to wear away like melting butter. The strength of steel had been sacrificed for a softer ride.

Finally, someone came up with a brilliant idea. If the steel's toughness could be wedded with rubber's ability to give a smooth ride, the result would be the perfect tire. You know the rest of the story: Safe, cushioned, long-lasting, steel-belted radial tires were born.

When it comes to moving a marriage down the highway of life, Chuck and Barb Snyder have come up with an idea every bit as brilliant as the radial tire. In this book they show husbands and wives how to combine the steel-like strengths of one marriage partner with the soft, relational desires and skills of the other. The result is a marriage that has the stamina to endure the bumps and bruises of life, and yet also provides the softness and comfort of a fulfilling relationship.

In the face of what many have thought were "incompatible" differences, men and women have traded in what could have been a great marriage for another model. Chuck and Barb show a better perspective on those differences. They remind us of an often-forgotten truth that can keep your relationship going and growing for a lifetime: In diversity, there can be unity and strength.

If you can read only one book on marriage this year, I urge you to make it this one. As you take in its humor, penetrating truth, and heart-grabbing stories, you'll give your marriage durability as well as a comfortable ride on the road to marital satisfaction.

GARY SMALLEY

Introduction

(CHUCK:) It's Monday evening. I'm not the only one whose life comes to a halt for a few hours on this particular night of the week. Millions of other men hang on to every play and vicariously live out the touchdown runs, the third-and-long pass completions, and dramatic interceptions. It's Monday Night Football!

But then Barb wants to talk. I've asked her to try withholding communication with me until halftime, but here she is trying to get my attention on some piddly little detail like the furnace blowing up or the dog dying.

Why can't she get my attention? . . .

Stay tuned!

We have just arrived at the hotel for our quiet weekend together. Barb has packed enough clothes and everything else to last four weeks. After lugging the nineteen suitcases to the fourteenth floor, I've just got them ready to be unpacked when Barb says, "What's that I smell?"

What does she mean?

And what does it mean to my life? . . .

Stay tuned!

We finally carve out enough time to go together to a play we've been wanting to see. There are no assigned seats tonight in the quiet, intimate theater, so now comes the momentous decision: Where to sit. Naturally I want to honor Barb, so I ask her where she would like to sit. She, wanting to honor me, says "I don't care—where do YOU want to sit?"

Now, I'm into decisions, right? I have employees asking me all the time what to do next. So I do what I know well how to do: I make a decision. "Let's sit here."

Barb takes a glance at my selection, then says, "No, let's sit down front."

What does she REALLY want when she asks for my opinion?

Stay tuned!

I DON'T KNOW if you can relate to any of these events in your life, but these seemingly minor, unimportant happenings are the stuff of which marriages are made. The conflicts seem so meaningless on the surface, but when they add up on top of each other day in, day out, they create friction. Communication slowly becomes more strained. One of the partners becomes quiet, the other begins taking the offensive, and soon communication virtually grinds to a halt.

Barb and I would like to share some of our differences and how we learned to accept them in each other. We believe that *accepting one another's differences is one of the vital keys to having a harmonious marriage relationship.* It's important that we look at each other as different, rather than "wrong."

The only reason Barb and I have a message for you is that we have worked through our problems rather than trying to get out of them. That's the key!

Barb and I team-teach almost every time we are asked to speak somewhere. I recently went to my first women's retreat as the only man in attendance, because we wanted to present a whole picture. Too often a speaker comes from only a man's viewpoint or a woman's viewpoint. Since both men and women are complicated when viewed from the other sex, having both Barb and I up front helps the listener discover how his or her mate is "wired." Barb and I also have spoken to men's groups where she was the only woman there. We just find that people seem to relate better to what we say when both viewpoints are presented. I liken this process to two rivers flowing together. At the point where the channels meet there is splashing and foam, but after the initial "adjustment," the resulting river is stronger, wider and deeper than either of the two originals.

We're written this book in the same way we teach, giving both viewpoints so you'll be able to see how the World's Most Opposite Couple fits together.

And by the way, keep in mind that the problems and struggles we are sharing here represent only about ten percent of our relationship. The other ninety percent is wonderful. (We don't want to scare off any singles from getting married!) There have been times, of course, when sixty percent of our relationship was not what it should have been, but as we learned lessons through hard times, the good times became more frequent.

Marriage is beautiful, and we recommend it highly, even though about the only thing Barb and I have in common is that we were married on the same day.

Now come with us as we explain why we believe incompatibility is grounds for a GREAT marriage!

1

I Thought She Was Wrong

(CHUCK:) Marriage is one of those situations my generation just fell into—doing what came naturally. Almost everyone got married after college. That's just what you did. Then you started having babies right away. No one knew what caused babies way back in the olden days, so our son Tim was born ten months and four days after we were married. I thought it was Barb walking through a daffodil field or something. Ten months didn't sound long enough to my grandmother, who quietly counted the months on her fingers when we told her about Barb's pregnancy.

The only preparation Barb and I had for marriage was a Family Relations class in college. We actually spent more time planning the wedding cake than preparing ourselves for this lifetime relationship. I don't know what our school systems are doing on marriage preparation these days —probably talking about the sexual relationship a lot. That's a fantastic part of marriage but it's only a small part of the whole. There are a ton of marriage books being written today, both secular and religious, but I doubt whether people actually take the time to read them, so congratulations on getting this far.

Barb and I had some very important people come into our life at a critical time to help us change our relationship into one where we began growing, rather than retreating —people like Gary Smalley, Larry Burkett, Kay Arthur and Larry Wright. (A glance at the bibliography in the back of this book will give others proper credit.) In fact, I think it is ESSENTIAL that we have a third party in our lives to help us learn how to have a good relationship. Especially for men, this is not something we pick up easily on our own.

I don't necessarily mean going to professional counselors either. They have their place, but sometimes an interested friend is just as good if not better. So often counselors have problems of their own with which they haven't properly dealt. I know of at least one marriage counselor who left his wife, married another woman and is still counseling. I can't believe it! That's like me running out and robbing a bank so I could have a ministry to bank robbers. Maybe we can be your "third" person by way of this book as we share the insights we have gained by working through the struggles in our relationship as they came along.

Many people seem to feel that differences in marriage are simply to be endured. In fact, isn't incompatibility one of our culture's most frequent excuses for divorce? We've found that Barb's strengths tend to be my weaknesses, and my strengths tend to be her weaknesses. Each of us completes the other. On the other hand, some people have the MOST difficulty in their marriage when they are SIMILAR in their personality styles. This is especially true in the case of very self-confident people. Both of them feel they are "right" when a conflict comes up, so it is very difficult for either one of them to give in and allow the other person to be right. Sparks fly until one of them backs down.

It is not wrong nor strange to be the same, so don't panic if this is the case with you. We're just talking about the general principles we've noticed in counseling, and in our own relationship. Actually some personality traits work BEST if the couple is the same. We recently gave a temperament test to a couple who both scored "rigid." This means they both have to plan their lives in advance and they get along great. It's when a rigid person marries an impulsive spur-of-the-moment type that the problems begin. It can be a growing time, or a hurting time,—depending on how the differences are accepted.

> (BARB:) What we want to say over and over again is that it's okay to be different. And because of these differences there *are* going to be disagreements and conflicts. One of the benefits of this, however, is that when you come from different points of view and still agree on an idea, you just know it has to be good!
>
> The longer you are married, the more differences you will find. You don't raise children the same, you don't spend money the same. One person wants all the windows up when you go to bed, the other wants them closed. One wants to go to sleep with music, the other wants complete silence. Even if both want to listen to music, it will probably be classical versus country and western.

Just because Barb and I have gone through some communication struggles in our relationship and have passed through the crying stage into the laughing stage, does not mean we no longer have conflicts. Barb hates to cook the same thing over and over. I hate to try new things. We both sat at the table recently and felt sorry for ourselves because this will never change. When she tries something new, she wants me to run around the table twirling my napkin around in the air. When I don't have a second helping she feels bad. If I DO have a second helping, I feel bad. Not because she's not a good cook—she's a wonderful cook! It's just that our taste buds are so different. She HAS introduced me to some new tastes, but I usually like to go back to the same old thing.

We have a horrible time fitting into each other's schedule. I believe God wants us to be on time for things. So when we are in the planning stage Barb will ask me when I want to leave. I will say 10:30. She will say, "How about 11?" If she doesn't want to take my decision, why does she ask? I simply will never understand why she wants me to make a decision if she is going to change it. Must be in the hormones or something.

The big difference for us when we have a conflict now is that we have a name for it, and have more knowledge of what the other person needs in that particular area of our differences. Our reward isn't just a better marriage, but the chance to help other people going through some of the same things we have experienced—only they're sometimes still in the crying stage.

We are in the advertising business and have the privilege of being involved in the lives of people in the media. We also have many friends who are professional athletes. Like adopted parents we've had the opportunity to help many of them go through some of their own problems getting adjusted to marriage and kids.

For instance, two years ago there were sixteen babies born to members of the Seattle Mariner's baseball organization. Now you would think with a baseball father, Baby would sleep in until 10 A.M. or so because Dad came in so late the night before from the game. Not so! They wake up at 4 A.M. and cause everyone lots of stress. Of course I advise the wives not to bother their husbands with the baby until it's at least two years old. In fact, the wives should just go live with their mothers until then because men don't seem designed to handle dirty diapers or being spit up on.

Most of the pros we work with are married, but as we began serving as chaplains for the University of Washington Husky football team, we started having singles come into our life too. We discovered something we knew instinctively, but hadn't put in words. Most young people in a dating situation are looking for someone just like themselves. They are looking for similarities. They want someone who likes the same kind of music and food, likes to go the same places, enjoys the same sports, etc.

Let's say the young man loves boats. He spends every waking moment out sailing. When he meets his beloved and shares his interest in boats, she's excited! She wants to share this part of his life too. He likes it, so she assumes that she will too. Then she tells him about how her family always goes to the county fair each year. She especially likes the produce barn where they make pictures by arranging various types of fruit in patterns, and the handwork exhibit is a must. He says, "That sounds great." Where she goes, he wants to go too.

Then they get married, and find out that she gets SICK on the boat and thinks he spends way too much time out on the water anyway, and he thinks there is nothing as boring as fruit displayed in patterns. Besides, he went to a fair in 1976, so why would he want to see another one?

What happened? While dating they were wide open to each other, sharing dreams, desires, interests, judgments, values, and preferences. The boyfriend even went SHOPPING with her, which by the way, is the highest honor a man can give to a woman. They also spent time visiting and sharing their lives. During this time they both were dwelling on positives rather than on negatives. They both went along with each other's wishes just to honor the other person and value the relationship.

After they get married, one of them notices with some irritation that the other always leaves the toothpaste tube on the sink with the cap off. The other one wants to drop everything and go for pizza, but has to wait until his or her mate finishes some project before they can go. Pretty soon, they begin spending more time on the negatives than on the positives, and the relationship begins to slowly deteriorate. In fact, the woman often begins to notice this shortly after the couple is pronounced man and wife.

What most women don't know is that after you come down the aisle with your new husband and go to change your dress, he goes in for brain surgery. The doctor on duty at the church removes the communication lobe, the shopping lobe, the visiting lobe, and the listening lobe. He replaces those with a career lobe, a Monday Night Football lobe, and a hobby lobe (workshop, golf, tennis, TV—whatever the husband has on his list of preferences). All of a sudden he is a different man than the one you married just minutes ago. You expect your shining knight to continue talking with you as you snuggle on the blanket under the stars. You expect him to be excited about the state fair (or at least GO). You expect him to enjoy shopping with you as much as he used to while you were dating. When these things don't happen, you are devastated. Now he's off to his career, Monday Night Football, tennis or golf . . . and you wonder where he went. His eyes glaze over when you talk to him about your world. You look in there, but no one is home. He HATES to shop, and quickly makes plans to meet you in forty minutes while he takes off for the hardware store or book shop.

Besides, most men shop differently than you women do. A man tends to see what he wants, picks it up, takes it to the checkout counter, and he's gone. He is not into doing much comparing or checking other stores or brands. He just wants to get on with his life. You women, on the other hand, enjoy the PROCESS of shopping more than he does, so an important part of your approach is comparing, checking, and evaluating.

Vinod Chabra of the Hearst Feature Service wrote an article based on some studies by Cornell University and *Better Homes and Gardens* on men shoppers. Here are some of the things they found:

1. Men are 70.9 percent less likely than women to clip coupons.

2. They are impulsive. If something strikes them as interesting or challenging—be it yucca or ugli—consider it sold.

3. They know only two types of meat, hamburger and sirloin steak. Their seafood choice is usually lobster.

4. They don't read food ads, or bother with shopping lists.

5. They buy a lot of snacks, especially pretzels and chips.

6. Males don't bother with nutritional labels, are quick to substitute, and aren't fussy over expiration dates.

7. They don't squirrel away sale items. Even toothpaste and toilet paper are purchased on an as-needed basis.

8. They are far more brand-loyal, avoid comparison shopping, and reach for the best, even when it comes to pet food.

I long ago gave up the idea of shopping with Chuck. When he goes with me, I feel this great pressure to hurry up and get done, and I can't really shop the way I want to. So I'm thankful when he goes off to his hardware store or book counter.

Gary Smalley told us of a shopping trip he took with his wife, Norma, to get a blouse—Gary thought he would go along as a way to honor her. Soon after arriving at the store, he picked up a blouse and said, "How's this?" (Not the right color.) "How about this one?" (Sleeves not right.) "You'd look great in this one!" (Too many stripes.) Then she picked up a *dress*. "We're not here to get a dress," proclaimed Gary. Then Norma wanted to stop for coffee. "*Coffee*? We're here to get a *blouse!*"

Gary explained that in going shopping, most men are out to conquer—take that hill, win that game, buy that blouse. To most women, on the other hand, shopping is more of a process than a goal.

The longer you're married the less you sweat the little things, like shopping together. I realize that during the first few years of marriage you want to do everything together, and that's great. But as the years go by and you relax a bit more, all you have to do is synchronize your watches and each go your own separate way in the mall. I don't get much joy looking at women's shoes, and Barb really isn't into what grit to get on sandpaper.

It takes work to have a harmonious relationship. It isn't 50-50, as we so often hear, but rather 100-100. Both partners must give all of themselves to the other, and become servants and ministers to each other. We come into marriage wanting *my* way, and think our mates will fulfill all our needs. It takes effort to focus on the other person's needs. Our natural tendency in marriage is to drift apart. It's easy to go our own way.

A good marriage is *forged* rather than simply *formed*. It is forged in the furnace of trials we go through together, and in the heat of tensions and conflicts that we recognize and work through.

The thing we as couples love most about each other in a dating situation soon becomes our greatest irritation after marriage. Chuck saw this friendly, outgoing person in me, and I saw his quiet, gentle spirit. But after we were married, he would think, *Good grief, does she have to talk to everyone?* And I had to learn that when Chuck got angry he didn't talk for three days. When I got angry I wanted to get it over with, and be friends, so I pursued—

You mean ATTACKED!

I just wanted to deal with it right then, but Chuck thought I was attacking him. I had a hard time with that. Chuck's way of handling conflict is a little more dignified than my way. He prides himself on being categorized as "submissive" according to a temperament test we took. What he overlooks, however, is that when he answered the same questions about me, he graded me more submissive than himself. The truth is that neither of us is submissive inside ourselves. We may act it out, but we are being submissive in some circumstances only because the Bible tells us to be.

Chuck *is* submissive when it comes to conflict, but that's the only time. It's just easier for him to give in than argue. We have since taken another test where he scored *very* dominant!

Lovingly dominant.

Dominant! And I was rated as being compliant.

Compliant to your own way of doing things.

You're right. I want things done a certain way, and he wants things done a certain way. When you have two people in a relationship who feel they are "right," then you are bound to have sparks. In fact, one marriage counselor told us we had the hardest type of relationship—two dominant people in the same match.

I happen to be more "right" than Barb because I'm President of the World. This means I get irritated when I'm in a hurry and someone else uses MY freeways, crowds into MY bank lines, fills up MY restaurants, or puts a construction detour on MY street. Let's face it, reader: YOU get in my way sometimes, and this irritates me a great deal.

Some of the differences we talk about in this book are

cultural, and some reflect different personalities, temperaments, and heredity. The type of parenting we received also
plays a part. However there ARE some God-designed differences between men and women that make us come at
things differently, and we'll talk about these later.

I know the idea of inherent male-female differences
bothers some of our feminist friends, but we hope they'll
have an open mind as they hear us out. Actually, the
women's movement has been responsible for some good
things in our society—more equal pay in the marketplace,
and more management opportunities, better working con-
ditions, and more respect for women. A woman corporation president should have the same pay, privileges and
perks that a man would have in the same position. Where I
think some people get off track, however, is trying to make
men and women the SAME. We can be equal, but we'll
NEVER be the same.

And by the way, if men had been doing what they
should have been doing in their marriages down through
history, the women's liberation movement would have been
unnecessary—just as there would be no need for unions if
management had not taken advantage of the workers, and
our race riots would never have happened if the white majority had shown genuine love and respect to our black
brothers and sisters.

This has been a man's world—no doubt about it—and
women have just barely begun to get the respect they de-
serve. But the fact will always remain that men and women
are different in so many ways.

Dr. Joyce Brothers has written a book pointing out a
host of differences between the sexes, including these:

• Men change their minds more often than women.

• Men snore more and fight more.

• Men have thicker skins and longer vocal chords.

• Men have redder blood—20% more red blood cells,
which means they have 20% more oxygen capacity.

- Men's daylight vision is better.
- Men's metabolic rate is higher.
- More men than women are left-handed.
- Men feel pain less than women.
- Men age earlier, but wrinkle later.
- Men lose weight more easily than women.
- Rich men are fatter than rich women.
- Men talk about themselves less, but worry about themselves more.
- Men and women's brains are even wired differently. (We'll talk about this more in detail later.)

Even magazines recognize a difference between men and women. Women's magazines deal mostly with relationships and matters related to the home—marriage, motherhood, children, sex, food, fashions, furnishings, medicine, psychology, and so on. Women want to understand themselves, their mates, and their children.

Men's magazines, on the other hand, are more performance oriented. There are many articles on setting records of some kind. There is less emphasis on relationships. They reflect that men's interests center around cars and around sports like boxing and football rather than ice skating. Men enjoy stories about war, spy action, adventure, business dealings, and of course sex—but mostly sex with a visual orientation rather than in the context of a relationship.

A man can be stimulated by a picture of a nude woman, but he has no idea whether she eats with her hands, has bad breath, or has had nineteen husbands. All he knows is that she looks good. On the other hand, women want to know about a man's family, his habits, his sensitivity, and his character. It's not so important how he looks, even though that is a factor. It's just not the most important one.

Whether these differences are hereditary, cultural, environmental, or God-designed doesn't really matter much. What does matter is that the two partners learn to ACCEPT the differences, in order to have a harmonious marriage relationship.

When Barb and I began giving our marriage seminars on accepting differences, we sat down and listed all the differences we had. We quickly found out something we already suspected: We are the World's Most Opposite Couple. We soon filled up a single spaced piece of typing paper. We have started a second sheet, but we'll only give you page one because we have lots of other things to talk to you about.

Each difference is really quite minor in and of itself, but as the differences accumulate, they become sources of irritation. The primary reason we offer these differences is to give you HOPE! If we can make it, YOU can make it. Here are some of the ways in which we are different:

(BARB:) *I like butter.*
(CHUCK:) I much prefer margarine.

I'm a low-energy person.
I'm a high-energy person.

I like my apple sauce hot.
I like ice crystals in my apple sauce.

I like my honey thin.
I like my honey just on the verge of turning to sugar.

I like jam with fruit lumps.
I like jelly because jelly has no lumps.

I'm relationship-oriented.
I'm goal-oriented.

I'm left-handed.
I'm right-handed. However this is an advantage in hotel bathrooms. All the towels, glasses, toothbrushes, etc. on the right side are mine. Those on the left are Barb's. It works great!

I like brown, nutritious, heavy bread full of seeds, nuts, soy flour, wheat germ, extra milk, and so on.
I like the white fluffy bread that builds strong bodies twelve ways—the kind you can roll up into little balls and throw at each other. The problem with Barb's bread is that you can't get up from the breakfast table if you have more than one slice because of all the rocks, sand and molasses in it.

I'm practical.
I'm a dreamer.

I love cooked vegetables.
I HATE cooked vegetables. If God had wanted us to eat cooked vegetables, he would have GROWN them cooked. In II Samson 3:2 it says, "Cursed is the cook who boileth the weed in its own juice, and crammeth it down the throats of the brethren" (csv).

I want my toilet paper to come off the top of the roll.
This has never been a very high priority with me, but when I am in the men's room at an airport or hotel I change the rolls just in case Barb ever goes in there.

When I listen to music, I like a background of soft violin strings.
I like the LOUD strings of country music. If the neighbors wouldn't complain, I'd have my garage made into a speaker.

(When I first met Chuck he had a western band called "Chuck's Chucklers," and he worked his way through

college playing music for granges and campus groups.
I would go with him and sit and listen, and just loved
being there. For years he took me to hear singers who
came to town like Ronnie Milsap, Connie Smith, Merle
Haggard, and Willie Nelson. He really enjoys their en-
tertainment, but they all sound the same to me. I liked
the music when Chuck was playing and singing it, but
not when someone else was. After twenty-five years of
marriage, I decided I didn't want to go to the shows
anymore, and asked him to take our son Tim or someone else instead—I had sacrificed enough!)

It's hard for me to make decisions.
It's easy for me to make decisions.

I like a variety of food.
I like the same old thing. If you find something you like,
stick with it! At several restaurants in Seattle the waitresses
begin my salad when they see me coming through the door.
They have warned me to call ahead if I ever want to change
my order, but why in the world would I change if I already
know what I like?

I like to be very accurate with details.
I tend to exaggerate at times.

*I come from a loud family where we sometimes shouted at
each other, but were friends again quickly.*
In my quiet family we NEVER shouted at one other, but
sometimes we wouldn't feel like speaking for a while.

I want to resolve conflict immediately.
I want to avoid conflict immediately.

I want to talk when I'm angry or we have a conflict.
The LAST thing I want to do is talk when I'm angry or we

are having a conflict. In fact, since you've finished your dinner, I can tell you I equate talking during a conflict with vomiting! I hate to get to it, but I DO feel better after it's over.

> *I'm not in the least threatened by teary TV programs or books.*

There are enough tears in the world. I like to laugh.

> *I plan for things to go right.*

I always have a Plan B. Plan A hardly ever goes right.

> *I believe stoplights were ordained by God to help bring order into our lives.*

I believe stoplights are a tool of Satan to disrupt my schedule.

> *I take main roads when I drive the car.*

I take shortcuts. My concern is to keep the car moving at all times.

> *I like to sit and read on vacations.*

I like to go and do and sightsee.

> *I'm a perfectionist.*

I'm disorderly.

> *I love clothes and have pretty good taste.*

I could care less about clothes. The only taste I have is in my mouth.

> *I have a clean desk.*

I have a rolltop.

> *I like my coffee black.*

Pass the cream and sugar please.

I'd rather talk on the phone than write notes
I much prefer writing notes.

I like small intimate groups where we can share deeply.
I like LARGE intimate groups where we DON'T have to
share too deeply.

I prefer just one or two pets—or maybe none.
I think Noah had a wonderful deal with two animals of
every kind. What a treat!

I don't mind sour things like lemons.
I have the world's biggest sweet tooth.

I'm a saver.
I'm a spender.

I'm a planner.
I'm impulsive.

I like Stevens Pass when we go over the mountains to visit
my folks. The scenery is beautiful—it looks like the Swiss
Alps.
The problem with Stevens Pass is that it has only two lanes,
and you get behind all those people who want to look at the
scenery—if you can imagine that. There are also 576 logging
trucks, 384 buses, 275 campers, and six people over 100
years old who want to drive fifteen miles an hour—and
they're all in front of me. Therefore I prefer Snoqualmie
Pass, where there are four beautiful lanes and I can get
around all those people and get on with my life. It took us
two weeks to go 150 miles the last time we went Barb's way.
How can I ever be a success if I'm spending that much time
sitting still?

I quickly stop and ask for directions when I get lost.
I feel that asking for directions is a sign of weakness. Just keep the car moving until you see this little halo over the address or a glow in the distance showing you the way. I don't like to stop and disrupt some guy's life at the 7-Eleven by asking "Where am I?" Sounds really dumb.

I feel comfortable taking things back to the store when they're not exactly what I need.
I have a garage full of things I should have comfortably taken back to the store.

I love healthy, nutritious food. The Good Earth is one of my favorite restaurants.
I much prefer McDonald's, Wendy's, Burger King, and Skipper's. I asked for bacon the last time we were at the Good Earth and we haven't been invited back since.

I take my time.
I'm always in a hurry trying to get something done.

I do one thing at a time, to conclusion.
I like to do many things at once, and once in awhile I might conclude something.

I hate paperwork.
I handle paperwork easily.

I'm pretty good at small talk and keeping a conversation going.
I hate small talk unless the person is contemplating suicide or divorce. Then we can talk about something important.

I prefer red clam chowder.
I prefer white clam chowder.

I endure to the end.
I like change. Why do the same thing for more than fifteen minutes?

I'm a good navigator.
I lose my way easily.

I prefer creamy peanut butter.
I prefer chunky peanut butter.

I like a very thin-lined ballpoint pen.
I like a broad stroke felt pen.

I like my toast almost burned.
I ask the cook to just breathe on it.

I prefer mayonnaise.
I prefer salad dressing.

I sometimes run my hair dryer on low.
I couldn't believe it. We were at one of our pro athlete conferences in Phoenix, and when I went to dry my hair I found the switch on low. How can our ship come in if we use our hair dryer on low? The thing to do is fire it up to super-high—close to a blowtorch—and dry your hair and get on with life.

I have been known to smash bugs in the house, and kill spiders that have fallen into the bathtub.
I carefully lift them out to safety on the back of an old envelope or something.

We don't have time to go boating, but if we did I would want a small, quiet sailboat.
I'm suspicious of people in sailboats sitting out there on the water waiting for a breeze. How can you be a success in life

that way? What I would want is a 90-horse Johnson so we could get where we're going. People in sailboats obviously have no goals in life.

Now doesn't that give you hope? I thought it would. We could probably stop this book right here and you'll have received your money's worth.

Accepting differences is one of the keys to a better marriage. Once again, this doesn't mean you're weird if you and your mate are the same—it just means that you have a different set of problems to work out.

2

Talk About Personality!

(CHUCK:) Two or three times a year, Barb goes to Wenatchee to visit her mom and leaves me to batch for myself. I think she does this to give me an idea of what she has to go through taking care of the house. I've been known to say something bright like, "What did you do today?" What's to keeping a house, right?

First of all, when I get up in the morning while she's gone, why would I make the bed? I'm just going to get back in it that night. It doesn't seem to be a good use of my time making it up every day.

Then there's the dishes. Why would I do the dishes? We have dishes in our cupboards that haven't been used since our wedding more than thirty years ago. Instead we keep using and WASHING the same ones. The plates in the front row are cracked and worn; the ones in the back row haven't been touched. So when Barb is gone, I just use the dishes and then stack them in the sink. I am very neat about it. I put all the plates together in one pile. I put all the saucers in one pile. I put all the cups in one pile. I put all the silver in a pan.

Just before Barb comes home, I put all the dishes in the dishwasher and make the bed. She's pleased, and I haven't been wasting my declining years making beds and washing dishes.

I'm not wrong, I just have a different personality style than Barb. Some great books have been written on this subject of personality differences. Florence Litteaur and Tim LaHaye are experts. We don't plan to redo what they have done, but would like to give you a simple overview and encourage a further look into the subject of personality differences to help you better understand your mate.

Basically there are four general personality types—the Analytical Person, the Driver, the Idea Person, and the People Person.

An Analytical Person likes structure. He or she is the one who writes the policy manual for the corporation—making sure it has even margins and the same number of lines on every page, and then making and sending copies to everyone else in the building.

The Driver person is the goal oriented, let's-get-it-done type who, if not careful, can run over people. He or she might call the Analytical person on the phone to ask, "Is the report going to be ready on Monday?" Analytical responds "No, I don't have any figures from the public relations department yet." "Use our budgeted estimates— they're close," suggests the Driver. "They wouldn't be exact," says Analytical. "But I need the report now," says Driver. The Analytical wants things done right—the Driver wants things done right away. Most business conflicts take place between the Analytical accountant and the CEO Driver.

Let's use a business situation as an example of how the four basic types work together. Let's say you have a report to give at an upcoming board meeting on a proposed new work project. You send out draft copies of it beforehand to everyone the project would involve. After a few days, you call Analytical and ask if the numbers in your report are right. Not only has Analytical read your report, but he has also made lots of neatly written comments in the margin. He can't imagine where you got all the wrong figures, and gives you the right ones.

Next you call Driver and ask if he could carry out the extra work from the new project. Driver says he can add some equipment or people, and assures you that with the additions it will work fine.

Then you call the Idea person, who convinces you to add in a few new features and systems to the proposal, and then says, "Now it will work."

Then you seek out the People person. You find him in the coffee shop relating to people. He hasn't read your report, but tells you of some people he thinks you should talk with before finalizing the proposal.

Then comes the day of the meeting. Your report is given and it gets unanimous approval—everyone applauds because everyone has had a say in it. Just imagine what would have happened if you had taken your report in cold. You would still be bleeding.

Another way to look at these different personalities is to see how they would take a trip. Analytical maps out the exact route, and knows where they'll stop for lunch each day and where they'll stay each night. He's also put together a budget, plus an ordered list—by highway number—of the roads to take. He has all this recorded in a notebook.

The Driver person also takes along a map, but wants to go six hundred miles the first day. "We've got to keep going. We can't make Coulee City if we keep stopping to eat or to see where Custer crossed the road or to visit all the antique shops."

The Idea person tries taking shortcuts by roads that barely make the map.

The People person has no map, and just heads in the

general direction of where they want to go, stopping along the way to ask someone where they are.

Another way of viewing our personality differences is to recognize what are called Type A people and Type B people. Type A's are goal-oriented. They're driven by the clock and set unrealistic deadlines for themselves. They are restless and always need to be doing something, and they hate red lights, stop signs, and bank lines. Type B people, on the other hand, take life more as it comes. They are more laid back and not so clock-driven, and they treat deadlines more as guidelines. They are more easily content, and able to just sit and read. They don't mind red lights, stop signs or bank lines because—more so than Type A's—they enjoy the simple process of living.

You can probably guess which of these last two types I am. Doctors have found out that we Type A's are more prone to heart attacks and other medical problems principally because of the way we handle stress and anger. Personally, I have put off my heart attack. I realize it is fashionable to have one around my age, but I've seen lots of hospital rooms and there is no way such a tiny area could hold my secretary's desk, all my file cabinets, and six phone lines. Besides it would be too awkward typing on that little tray they put across your chest. So I think I'll just postpone the attack for a while (even though you do get lots of attention and love during recovery) and leave it to others with more time.

Besides, if I ended up in the hospital I don't think Barb could take care of my animals. It's very complicated. When I come home from work I first feed the two white cats, because if I feed Stranger (another cat) first, the white cats chase her away from the food and she'll starve in the woods. So I feed the white cats in the back yard, and while they're eating, I rush around front and give Stranger the instant dinners she likes so much. I have to be careful not to let out our dog Muffit yet, because she loves to eat the cats' food, both back yard and front. As soon as I get the cats supplied and the bird feeder filled, Muffit is barking from hunger. I put Alpo in her dish, which she doesn't eat yet because she wants a dog treat first. She loves jerky treats, and has a couple of those. I still can't let her out because as soon as Stranger and the white cats finish eating, Calico cat comes up to eat. (She's quite wild and won't come around when everyone else is eating.) Then there's Rabbit, a wild little cutie that came out of the woods to live with us. I take her carrots and make sure she has plenty of alfalfa pellets. I have to make sure I put out plenty of food everywhere, because after everyone has eaten, the raccoons come out of the woods and finish up.

So you see, if I went to the hospital a whole bunch of furry people would starve to death, and I can't have that on my conscience.

Another way Barb and I differ is in the area of impulsiveness. I tend to change my mind quite often. I'll be going one way, and here comes Barb right along with me. Then all of a sudden I'll change directions and she'll wonder, "Where did you go? I thought you were going *that* way." "That was last week," I reply. "This week I am going THIS direction." It drives her out of her mind. I guess she feels insecure because she has no idea which direction I'll head next. She gives me the feeling that once I choose a path, I should follow it the rest of my life. But who wants to go the same direction all the time? I get bored easily. I need variety. Besides, being impulsive never hurt anyone, at least from my standpoint. It seems quite natural to me.

(BARB:) Let me tell you about living with an impulsive person. Chuck has bought every piece of exercise equipment known to man because he was going to look like a football player in two weeks. Each piece was something he just *had* to have—I wasn't so sure it was all that important, but to Chuck it was the most

> important thing in the world, and once he got it he
> was going to use it every day for the rest of his life.

I never said that. Just because I bought the stuff was no
guarantee I would use it for the rest of my life. After two
weeks of hard work and noticing no change in my figure, I
put it aside until some other day when I have more time. If I
can't look like a football player in two weeks then let's get
on to something else that will produce faster results.

I guess that's one of my biggest problems—wanting instant results. Almost every year on the second day of January (I don't want to ruin dinner on New Year's) I resolve
to get in better shape. I make out a plan to do forty pushups
each morning and pump iron for an hour afterward, plus
forty more pushups before I go to bed at night. I also plan to
go each day to Green Lake and run six miles. I do this for
two days religiously, but when I see that the mirror does not
reflect a difference in my fallen chest, I reward myself for
the good effort with some pizza and ice cream, and get on
to something a little more practical—like going to work.

> Chuck bought a Universal Gym, and after buying it
> found it was too tall to put in our basement, so he had
> to have an exercise house built which cost thousands
> more than either of us had imagined—something
> about a sliding hillside or something. Now we have
> this fabulous exercise house that he hasn't used for a
> year.

That's not true. I clearly remember going in there within the
last six months—for some bird seed I keep there. As I was
saying before Barb interrupted, being impulsive is not bad.
I have a stamp collection with all the plate blocks and individual stamps I've saved since high school. I have all the
stamp albums I need to put them in too. Someday I'll put
the stamps in the books.

I also collect coins, but they are still in cans even though I have the coin books. I'll get to it presently. My impulsiveness makes it hard for me to put the little plastic tab back on the bread wrapper to keep the bread fresh. Or to take the fringes off postage stamps before I lick and affix them to envelopes. How in the world is my ship ever going to come in if I keep taking fringes off stamps and putting tabs on bread wrappers? I need to keep moving.

Sometimes for breakfast I have a combination of wheat germ, peanut butter and honey. Barb complained because there were drips of honey coming down the side of the jar after I put it away, which made the cupboard shelf sticky. So I just got a plastic dish and put the honey jar in that. The cupboard stays unsticky, and I get on with my life rather than spend my twilight years wiping off jars of honey.

Instructions are another thing I tend to disregard because of the time it takes to read them. While Barb is a ready-aim-fire type of person, my philosophy of life tends to be ready-FIRE!-aim. For instance, I put up a metal shed at our cabin. What is there to putting up a little metal building, right? Four walls, a roof, a door, and you're done. Who wants to take the time to read the directions? So I put it up—no big deal. When I stepped back to admire my work, however, I noticed a little bag of leftover white things. I whipped through the instruction book looking for "white things" and found that they were the rubber washers I should have put under the 592 screws that hold the roof together and keep it from leaking. Here in Seattle that IS a problem, but being a true impulsive I just grabbed my caulking gun and zapped all the screws, and the shed didn't leak. It didn't look too good, but our guests never went into it anyway, except maybe the kids—and they understand. Besides, I needed to get on with my life.

I've started reading 2,974 books. I've finished several. I also keep quite a few stacked by my side of the bed. If I want to go to sleep I read history. If I want to stay awake I read a spy novel. If I want to learn something, I read one of Chuck Swindoll's or James Dobson's latest books. There is one little problem, however: Our insurance does not cover Barb while she is making my side of the bed. They think it's just too risky for her to step over all those books.

I've always wanted to take speed writing and reading, but haven't been able to work them into my schedule yet. Barb gave me a speed tape recorder I wanted for my birthday. This plays tapes at twice the normal speed so I can get on with my life. I haven't had time to use it much yet, but I'll be glad to have that convenience someday when I get around to it.

Actually I have used it a couple of times. Barb teaches this wonderful Bible study series by Kay Arthur called *Precept upon Precept*. Kay Arthur's ministry is headquartered in Chattanooga, Tennessee, and has a worldwide outreach. Sometimes we use this material in our Bible study groups for pro-athlete couples. I do the overview and Barb leads the discussion, but once in a while I have to fill in for her. To prepare, we listen to *Precept upon Precept* leader's tapes, which are recorded by Betsy Bird. She's a sweet little southern belle with a beautiful drawl, but because she tends to draw out her words and speak a little slower than we folks do in the West, I put her on my speed tape recorder and crank it up to twice the normal speed, and it works great. She sounds like a Type A from Seattle.

By the way, if you wear glasses, here's an impulsive idea that will help pay you back for buying this book. When I first started to wear glasses, I noticed I had to wash them every three to four days if I wanted to see. So somehow I was conned into buying those little spray bottles that hold .00089 ounces of fluid (about eight or ten sprays) and cost five bucks or so. Later I decided to get a quart of Windex from Safeway and put a sprayer on top. In the morning I bathe my glasses in Windex and get on with my life. One bottle should last fourteen years and I figure I'll have saved about $7,129 by not buying the little spray containers.

Now some of you are thinking that Barb must be perfect, if she is the opposite of me. Well, she's not so perfect. (In communication circles this is called "counterattack.") Take her pantry, for instance. You have to be very careful, because the potatoes have long sprouts on them that reach out and trip you—deliberately. Sometimes a green feeler grabs at me from one of the Tupperware dishes holding leftovers in the refrigerator, and the apples grow fuzz.

Barb's folks have fruit trees at their home, and they used to load up our car trunk when we visited. We really appreciated their thoughtfulness, but we never quite got around to using all the fruit before it rotted. I would take the fruit from the trunk to the garage, then a few months later I would take the fruit to the garbage can. I once suggested to Barb that it would be lots more efficient if I just took the boxes directly from the trunk to the garbage. It would save all that storage. She didn't quite see it that way.

I also remember the time we were bumped up to first class on one of our trips. We've never felt the extra money was worth the prestige, but we were excited when we found ourselves up in the linen-napkin compartment. A tragedy happened, however, Barb dropped her dinner roll on the floor, and we've never been asked back since.

Barb is delaying a lot of fun things we could be doing as a couple. For instance, we can't go on the 25-mile survival hike until she picks out the color of backpack she wants. We can't take the July drive through Death Valley in the four-wheeler until she decides whether we should get a Dodge or Ford. I have plans for an amusement park called "Chuckland," but Barb can't decide if she wants to make jelly in the mornings (like Knott's Berry farm) and take tickets in the afternoon, or tickets in the morning and jelly in the afternoon. Until she makes these critical decisions, I guess we'll just have to stay home.

And here's the most serious flaw in her character. It's

the reason I could never run for President of the United States, as the reporters are sure to dig out this skeleton from our closet: Barb is addicted to Haagen-Dazs Rum Raisin Ice Cream. She has even been known to—hang on to your hat—eat a whole pint at one sitting. I can see the headlines now: *EXTRA! EXTRA!* CANDIDATE SNYDER WITHDRAWS FROM PRESIDENTIAL RACE DUE TO WIFE'S ADDICTION.

See? She's not so perfect.

> It isn't easy living with a type A, impulsive, driver-type person, but at least it keeps life interesting. Frustrating at times, but interesting. Chuck used to give me a list of goals to accomplish. I'd get one or two done and want to savor the accomplishment, but he'd say, "When are you going to get this other project done?" or "How's that one coming?" He wasn't even enjoying what I had finished!

What is the logical thing to do when you've accomplished a goal? Set another, of course. But Barb wants to rest, if you can believe that.

> That's right. I do want to rest. It's an important part of the whole process of getting something done, a process that I enjoy more than Chuck does. He just wants to get it done and get on with something else.
>
> Another word for impulsive is changeable. When Chuck comes up with an idea and tells me about it, he makes me feel it's the most important thing in the world to him. He has sold me on it with every ounce of his conviction. I think about it, decide to go along with the idea, and make my adjustment to his way of thinking. Then I find out he's decided it's not a good idea after all and is headed in a different direction.
>
> Impulsive people feel they have the best idea

around, and have to do it *right now!* Not only that, it often involves money. That's okay if you can afford it, but often you can't. For nine years I waited to buy a new carpet for the first home we owned. This was when Chuck was starting his production company for radio and TV commercials. I was keeping the company's financial books, and could tell when we would have almost enough money to buy the carpet—but just then he would have an idea for another new piece of business equipment.

Once it was an electric organ for musical jingles. As he often did, he said to me, "It's for you—it's for the business." Somehow it never seemed like it was for me. Of course he thought it was for me because he is my provider, but I really thought he could provide best for me by letting me buy a new carpet. I finally agreed that he should buy the organ, but then I noticed that he used it for only one or two commercials. It wasn't long before he had another idea to buy something else "for the business."

A friend of ours, author and financial counselor Larry Burkett, has what he calls his 30-day plan for purchases. He loves tools, but when he sees a tool he just *has* to have, he makes himself wait thirty days before buying it. By the time thirty days is up, there is something else he just has to have. This is how he controls his impulsiveness.

We've mentioned another friend, Gary Smalley, who is almost a carbon copy of Chuck in the area of dreaming and impulsiveness. When Gary and his family come for a visit, he and Chuck always have what they call their "noncompleters" lunch. This means they don't take Norma and me along. They can dream and plan and solve the world's problems without anyone saying, "How will you pay for it? . . . Where will you park it? . . . Have you thought about this? . . . What about that?" and other practical things that come to a woman's mind.

Once Gary asked Chuck if we could come to a conference and give a temperament test to a group of business leaders. Chuck was very excited and decided this would be a great thing to do. Then I called Norma and asked a few questions. "How long is the conference?" (Two and a half days.) "How many people will be there?" (Three hundred.) "Norma, we can't grade, chart and analyze the test for that many people in two and a half days." As Norma reported these facts to Gary I could hear him in the background saying, "Oh, yeah—I guess we won't have time." The two men were all set to do this impossible task because they had their eyes on the goal, while Norma and I on the sidelines were thinking through the process.

It's vital that each of us knows what personality style our mate has. There are a variety of tests that can determine this. The Taylor-Johnson test is one of the best. When we know the strengths and weaknesses related to the various personality styles, we can be more tolerant of our mates and say, "That's just the way they are!"

3

Nice Putt!

(CHUCK:) Men, have you ever been working in your workshop and find you need a few screws or nails or some tool at the hardware store? I have. Often I'll decide to make a super-quick trip to the hardware store and plan to get back pronto. I then make a big mistake: I mention my plan to Barb. All of a sudden my goals are altered. Now I am stopping by the supermarket for some milk, at the cleaners to pick up a skirt, and at the garden shop for some bedding plants, plus a quick trip across town to deliver a birthday present. My whole life comes screeching to a halt, and I am lucky if I ever get back to my shop that day.

(BARB:) We women don't mean to mess up our husband's goals. We just think that as long as he is out, he might as well save us a few steps.

Women have goals too, but our goals tend to be more relationship-oriented. Usually they have some-

thing to do with our home and friendships. Even
when a woman works in the marketplace, her goals in
the forefront of her mind often include concerns for
her family like: Is the house clean? Do I have enough
food in the refrigerator? Are the clothes washed and
put away?

Since women are more into relationships, they
spend more time simply sharing their lives with other
people. A frequent goal for a woman is just to spend
time with a friend or family member or perhaps someone in need.

When women go out for lunch they may have no
other plans than to share their lives with each other.
When men go to lunch, it's usually to solve a business
problem, get acquainted with a potential client, or just
satisfy their hunger before or after playing golf or
tennis. Their talk is usually about what they're *doing*,
while women talk more about their relationships and
what they're *feeling*.

You say men don't share their lives with each other? Well
you're wrong. We do a lot of that when we're together. For
instance, when we play golf we talk all the time: "Nice
putt" ... "Hooking a little bit today, aren't you?" ... "Watch the
rough on the next hole" ... "Find your ball?" ... "Way to go!"

I guess that's proof that when we share our lives,
men and women don't share the same thing. When
women are eating out, the waitress comes forty-five
minutes after they've been seated, and they haven't
even looked at the menu yet. The first thing a group of
men are likely to do is take the menu and decide what
they'll order, and then they begin talking.

When I'm at church alone, I look for a person I
know to sit with, because I want to share the experience with someone. When a man goes to church alone,

he just goes in and sits down. His goal is to attend church, and that's what he does.

Each Sunday when the church service ends, Chuck's goal is to go home and get on with his life, while mine is to stay around and talk. So we've compromised. Chuck goes out to the car and listens to Chuck Swindoll tapes or reads a book while I stay inside and catch up on my relationships. It's not that he doesn't like people, but that his comfort zone is in the car.

On the other hand, when we go to a retreat to speak, it just amazes me to see Chuck going around from table to table or person to person to welcome those who've come and make them feel comfortable. He has a goal to touch people's lives, and he is in control of the situation. When he's at a party or reception or some other social event where he is *not* in charge, he dislikes making small talk.

I'm just not good at small talk. Did you see the paper this morning? Evidently terrorists have come up with a new diabolical torture method for hostages. They have a simulated front room with coffee tables and overstuffed chairs. They march the prisoners into the room, sit them down, and force them to make small talk! Their minds snap in twenty to thirty minutes. By the way, another horrible torture the terrorists have is a simulated football stadium where they march the prisoners in, sit them in the stands, and then just have one long continuous halftime—with high school marching bands. The prisoners are blithering idiots in no time.

I realize I should learn to be more outgoing and conversant, so I am trying—but it's still hard.

Chuck *is* getting better . . . but just sitting and visiting is still not his favorite thing to do.

Since women tend to be more relationship-oriented

than men, they have a harder time pulling up and moving to another area. Their roots go deeply into family, friends, church and community. A woman worries about making new friends, and leaving her family, and not being able to see the kids grow up in the church she knows so well. How will they find the right church home after they move? And where will she find the right doctor? What school will the kids go to, and will it be as good as the one they now attend? How will she maintain relationships with the friends she is leaving behind? On the other hand, a man is interested in his new job, and how it will advance his career. Besides, he feels the most important people —his wife and children—are coming with him anyway, so he can just pick up and go.

We changed churches a few years ago because Chuck felt that was what God wanted us to do, and I thought so too. But it was much harder for me to leave the old church than it was for Chuck. He had a goal—to be obedient to the Lord. I had many friends in the church we were leaving, and I didn't know anyone at the new church. It was one of the hardest things I have ever done. True friends do indeed remain friends no matter where you go, but I didn't know that at the time. I still do not get to see my old friends as much as I want to, but I would miss my new friends just as much if the Lord ever told us to leave our present church.

We have many friends on the Seattle Mariners baseball team. I believe this sport is the hardest one on family life. In football, the men go away for two days, and then come home. In baseball the players may be on the road for as many as sixteen days at a time. Because of all the time spent without their husbands, the baseball wives plan many activities together, and their friendships become very close. As professional athletes the men have a goal—to play baseball. The women have a goal too, and it's to form close relationships that will get them through the days until the person who represents her closest relationship comes home.

There can also be big differences in the way a man and woman come home from work. The man comes home tired, and just grabs his newspaper or flips on the TV and seemingly *never* feels like chatting; or at least he says he needs lots of "space" to recover from his day. If his wife is returning from her job outside the home, she's also very tired—but within a half an hour or so she's usually ready to talk about her day. Even if his wife is a fulltime mother and homemaker, she definitely wants some adult talk after a day of "Ma-Ma" and "more-ice-seem-peez."

This business of "re-entry" on the part of the husband is critical. He thinks if he sits down with his wife to talk and share the day, his whole evening will be taken up with it. What actually happens when he gives his wife some time to explore their days together is that she releases him rather quickly to do something else. She just wants to be involved in his world, and does not appreciate it when she asks him, "How did work go?" and he responds only with, "Fine."

I was explaining this principle to our son, Tim, who manages a diesel shop. I told him that his wife Tammie needed to be a part of his world when he came home. Even though she is not a diesel mechanic, I suggested the next time she asked how his work went that day, he should say something like, "Well you know that 236 engine we've been working on? We dropped the pan on that baby and found all kinds of iron shavings. That of course meant the bearings were shot. I had Charlie come take a look because he's our bearing man, and while he was working on it, he took off the head and noticed a few burnt valves. That delayed us several hours getting the job done, but we . . ." etc.

Tim couldn't believe she would be interested in all that. I said, "Trust me." So he went into lots of detail the next time she asked how his day was, and he also cleaned the basement on his own. He later reported in a letter to me that as a result, Tammie lavished him with kisses. She was glad he valued the relationship enough to share his world with her, as well as doing something for her without being asked.

We've learned that intimate conversation is every bit as important to a woman as sex is to a man. But because the two people involved don't know this, there are lots of misunderstandings. The man doesn't put himself out to listen and share, and the woman thinks he's a beast because he wants to go to bed all the time but hasn't shown much interest in the relationship outside the bedroom. Yet if we focus on our mate's needs and fulfill them, he or she will often turn around and fulfill ours.

We were in Phoenix at one of our pro-athlete conferences a few years ago, and had an hour to kill before the first meeting. I suggested to Barb that this would be a great time to visit and talk. She said, "I think I'll read the paper." I took that as a great compliment. Evidently we were up to date in the talking department, so she was free to read the paper. I had filled her talking needs for that particular day.

Here's a great idea for you men to prove to your wives that you are sensitive and want to talk. Wait until Buffalo and Cincinnati play each other in football on Monday Night Football. (For you folks in the East who LOVE Buffalo or Cincinnati, you can substitute Seattle and San Diego.) The point is to pick a game that does not interest you, and offer to take your wife out to dinner and to talk. Say something like, "You are so important to me that I'm going to skip Monday Night Football this evening. In fact, I'm not even going to tape it. I'm going to take you out to dinner instead. We have lots to talk about, and who cares about Monday Night Football anyway when I can be with you? I want to catch up on what's happening in your life." She may faint.

Don't worry—she'll recover quickly and you'll be her hero for the entire season. From that moment on, every time she sees you in front of the TV set watching football, she'll remember that special evening when you gave it all up for her.

Hopefully the results of his evening of talking will make him want to do it again sometime. It's really lots of fun—and vital to keeping a relationship fresh. If we don't make sure we talk to each other, something like this often happens: The wife tries for years to get her husband to talk to her, to pay attention to her, to see her as a worthwhile, interesting individual. When this doesn't happen, say after twenty to twenty-five years of noncommunication by the husband, she decides to get a job so she can get some approval somewhere. If she can't get approval at home, then maybe she can get it from a job.

At the same time, the husband has come to the realization that he will never be president of the company, so he decides that home and wife look pretty good after all. Just as he comes home for a relationship, she goes out the door to find a job. All she needed was a relationship that was not so one-sided, and some approval at home.

When the kids were growing up, Chuck and I always did our best communicating after dinner. There were usually children's shows on TV between 6 and 7 in the evening, so after dinner, the kids would leave the table to watch TV, the dogs would hop up on Chuck's lap, and we would talk about the day's events. This fulfilled my need for updated communication with him. Afterward Chuck was free to go to his workshop or do anything else he wanted to that evening, and I would read a book or do whatever I wanted to. The kids would come back in the kitchen and wash the dishes. Wasn't that good planning? Now that our family is raised, we still find dinner the best time to talk, but now it's often at a restaurant.

In his book *Passive Men and Wild Women*, Pierre Mornell explains that when a man comes home after work, the most important part of his day is over; he has provided for his family. His wife, on the other hand, is just beginning the most important part of her day—making contact with her husband. She wants to talk. He wants to be left alone because he has talked all day. She doesn't understand and gives him disapproval. He doesn't understand and resists her disapproval. She presses him to talk. He resists her more. Finally she goes to the telephone and calls a friend.

Days later when she once more tries to get her husband to talk, he says, "How can I talk to you when you're always on the phone?" That's when she becomes wild and hysterical, and he wonders what's wrong with her.

Dr. Mornell suggests that when a woman says, "Can we talk?" the man thinks he'll have to talk with her the whole evening. He feels as if he's being thrown into a swimming pool where he can neither swim nor climb out. He thinks he'll drown.

To overcome this situation, a good idea is for the couple to decide together on a time limit on talking. Even as little as ten minutes or so could go a long way in fulfilling the woman's needs. Actually it fulfills both their needs: her need to talk, and his need for some time by himself. The time commitment means they both have hope.

We women don't expect our husbands to fulfill all our needs for verbal communication. That's why we have lunches with friends, coffee with neighbors, and Bible studies together. Some of the best times of my life were when the children were small and my friends and I would get together to iron clothes, sew, can fruit or knit. This is something young women can enjoy even today.

One of the problems with women's groups is that they talk about husbands. And Barb, since she's usually the teacher, makes me one of her best examples of how not to do it. She was teaching on finances recently. I stopped by the church to leave off something and went to the door of the room just to wave hello. She saw me, called me in, and ninety women started laughing. I HAVE made a few mistakes in learning God's way of handling finances, but they weren't THAT bad!

Or I'll be innocently walking down the hall of our church and a strange woman will come up to me and say something like "YOU BEAST"—and huff along her way. I know then that Barb's been talking about me in her Bible study.

That's never happened. I'm very complimentary.

Well, maybe not yet, but it probably will one of these days.

At the church Barb and I attend we've started something that other groups might want to consider—and that's rotating one husband into the women's Bible Study each week. That way we have a representative who knows what really goes on. We don't ask a man to do that more than once every six to eight months, however, because all that personal sharing does take its toll.

These tendencies we've noted about women being more relationship-oriented and men more goal-oriented are not 100-percent true for everyone. There are many very sensitive, relationship-oriented men, and lots of driven, goal-oriented women. We're just talking about how men and women are usually designed. Don't panic if you're just the opposite.

Either way, neither one of the partners will fulfill ALL

the other's needs. As Barb mentioned, there is a definite need for the wife to have women friends, and equally important for the man to cultivate men friends.

Another piece of evidence indicating that women are usually more relationship-oriented than men can be seen when a couple goes to visit the wife's folks. She and her mom will hug and go into the kitchen to catch up on each other's lives. Her dad and the husband will shake hands, and go into the living room. Pretty soon the wife notices a lot of silence coming out of the living room. She looks in and finds her father and husband reading the paper or watching a sports event. They are not talking at all. She wonders whether her husband really LIKES her dad, because they are not talking. Actually they have a goal, and that is to watch the game on TV or read the newspaper. Most men don't need to talk a lot to have fellowship.

Curt Warner, running back for the Seattle Seahawks, became one of our "kids" shortly after arriving in Seattle. After about a year Barb asked him if he had gotten to know Jim Zorn very well. Jim was the quarterback on the team at that time. Curt said he hadn't—yet they had shared the same buses, airplanes, hotels, huddles, and locker rooms for a year. Barb couldn't believe it, but I could. Men can work toward a goal for years and never really get to know each other. That's why God created women, to help us learn how to relate better.

I even approach TV shows differently because I'm not as relationship-oriented as Barb. Take for instance the show *North and South* that ran a few years ago on TV. It was about the Civil War, one of my areas of interest. We were away from home when it aired, so I videotaped it for later viewing. As I was viewing it on tape I saw a couple grab their blanket and head for the lake. I knew I was in for twenty minutes of talking and sharing, so I used my remote and fast-forwarded the tape to the next battle scene. No use wasting my time watching people in a private conversation.

I've already mentioned that social conversing is not my long suit. When someone calls on the phone, it's an effort for me to talk beyond three or four minutes, unless of course they're in trouble or need my advice. I love to help people, but if it's just small talk, it's hard for me to keep a conversation going. On the other hand, Barb can talk an hour with the same person I talked with for a couple of minutes. When I ask Barb what they talked about, it's hard for her to relate everything in detail, but they did have a good time sharing.

If I have a goal like answering questions after a teaching session, or counseling someone over lunch or on the phone, I'm a great talker. Hopefully I'm a good listener too, but it is no effort to keep a conversation going when I have a goal. If it's just small talk to kill time, then I'm a terrible conversation partner.

Knowing that women are more relationship-oriented has helped me in traffic. It used to irritate me to get behind two women in a car. They just didn't seem to be as interested in getting to where they were going as I was. Now I know why. They were enjoying the relationship along the way to the goal. Since I understand that now, I can just be patient behind them—read my book, catch up on some paperwork, make some phone calls, and not get irritated. This is not a knock on women drivers, so save your cards and letters. This is just understanding that a woman is usually more into the relationship than the goal, and this is just the way women are designed. The sooner I learned to appreciate it rather than fight it, the better Christian I became behind the wheel of my car.

But let me be completely honest: One thing that irritates me to no end is yuppie dolls in their little sports cars riding my rear bumper with only a couple of coats of paint separating us—at sixty miles an hour. At this point sometimes I get a disease that has my doctor baffled. It's called unpressurizing tendonitis, and causes my gas peddle foot

to get a shooting pain which requires that I let up on the gas
a bit, which seems to slow down my vehicle, which seems
to irritate the woman behind me to the point that she roars
around me with her cute little nose holding her designer
sunglasses in the air as she curses the older generation.
Hopefully medical science will find a cure for this de-
plorable disease, but until then I guess I have to live with it.

Barb and I have been excited to see women named to
the President's Cabinet and appointed or elected to other
high government posts in Washington. I'm sure these
women provide the men with insights they otherwise
would not have . I can see it now: One of the men suggests
that we nuke South America, and one of the women says,
"Have you thought about this?...What if that happened?
...Do you really think it is necessary?"

Barb and I feel that if the top leaders of Russia and the
the United States were women, we wouldn't have to worry
about a war between the superpowers. War is a man's
thing. One of the women would say to the other, "You
mean, my missiles bother you? Well I'll give you ten if you
give me ten. How are the kids? Let's get together for
coffee." Two women would work out the relationship. It's
the men who want to "Take that hill," "Conquer that fort,"
"Stretch those boundaries."

> Because women are more relationship-oriented
> than men, we are also more emotionally responsive.
> We easily get caught up in the relationships of a good
> book or movie. Women are usually more open; men
> are usually more closed. There are emotional men too,
> but you don't often find a man crying over an emo-
> tional dialogue in a book or movie or on TV. Women
> *do* cry easier, and some of this has to do with a woman
> having more prolactin in her system than a man does.
> A man is usually more in control of his feelings and
> will often stuff them and walk away in silence. A man

might not hear a woman until she creates a crisis of some kind. Tears get the man's attention even though the tears might not be intentional.

Women are more able or willing to share problems with each other. You know, we women counsel each other all the time. We understand each other very well, and never think it's a negative if someone is having a problem. A man usually would never be caught dead sharing his problems. He wants to pretend he doesn't have any, and if he has some, it is his wife's fault. The wife almost always seeks marriage counseling before her husband does.

I remember early in our marriage Chuck saying, "I would never share my problems with anyone." I laugh now, because he is sharing what he has learned with almost everyone with whom he comes in contact. In fact, he even wrote a book about his failures, and everyone thinks he's wonderful because he is so real.

When a woman gets into a conflict she desperately wants to share what she is feeling, and to have some understanding from her husband. Instead of giving her understanding, the man will usually tell the woman to *do* something to get rid of her problem. The impression they give us is "Here are five easy steps to your crisis. What other little problem do you have?" We don't want solutions, we want understanding. When the man gives us solutions too quickly, it makes us feel like our problems aren't very important.

On our refrigerator is a cartoon showing two young people in front of a television. The girlfriend reminds her boyfriend that they've just seen the pregame warmup, the coach's preview, the predictions show, the starting lineups, the game itself with a hundred replays, the postgame show, the coach's wrapup, the locker room show, and the after-game call-in program—and now she just wants to talk with him about their relationship. "Isn't that just like a woman," he says. "Always wanting to REHASH everything."

Sometimes a husband will say to his wife, "You're just too sensitive," and it's true we are sensitive. We see and feel lots of things men do not. We know when all is not going well between us. I was aware that one couple in our life was having problems. The young wife was aware of it too. In fact, she had spoken to her husband about it many times over a period of months. It wasn't until she created a crisis that the young husband said, "I've thought for a couple of days there might be something wrong."

Women have a need for their relationships to be right with everyone. We're sensitive to others' needs and show it by being the driving force to get our men to go to weddings, funerals, anniversary celebrations and the like. We know when others need to be honored. I think, however, our husbands would rather watch golf or the NFL football game on TV, or go fishing.

For the first two hundred years after I get to heaven, I hope the Lord will be reshowing all the Super Bowls, World Series Games, playoff games, tennis championships, golf finals, and Final Four basketball games I've missed by being at all the social events I have gone to because Barb thought we should be there. And because He is God, He'll make it appear that the games are "live."

It's not that I don't want to honor the people involved. It's just that the events are so inefficient. Take weddings, for instance. The hosts should have the candles lit and the mothers seated when we get there. Then the rest of the wedding party should just come in one of the side doors instead of traipsing one by one down the aisle. The pastor should not try to give a sermon, but just say a simple "Do you take this man" type of thing, and then say, "Dismissed" at the end instead of filing out row-by-row wasting a great deal of time. Then we should just have the bride and groom read the guest book to see who was there, so we wouldn't have to go through the reception line. And let's not ruin people's lives by scheduling weddings at 2 P.M. on a perfectly good Saturday. Let's make a rule that no wedding can take place before 8 P.M. in the evening. We're adults; let's be realistic. The bride and groom are all wrapped up in each other anyway, so let's make it easy for everyone and have short, late-evening weddings. I have to get on with my life and can't waste my time waiting to be dismissed.

Also, wives, when another invitation comes in the mail to a wedding or graduation that the two of you simply can't miss, and your husband discovers it will mean misisng a long-awaited football playoff game on TV, please don't expect his instant acceptance. You see, he has to go through a grieving process. He might react negatively. Let him; he'll do the right thing when it gets down to it. He'll honor you. But it's such a shock to his cardiovascular system to contemplate going to weddings and graduations—it takes a process to bring him to the point of accepting this setback in his life. Be patient and don't expect instant approval. Let him grieve for a moment without condemnation.

Men are usually into *things* and *doing*, and women are into *persons* and *being*. Men like to count, weigh, combine and amass things. According to Paul Tournier in *The Gift of Feeling*, a man does this to increase his power. He talks about men judging an athlete's value to one-hundredth of a second, feeling there is no more irrefutable proof than figures. Women, on the other hand, will make up their minds on the attractiveness of his or her style. Descartes said, "I think, therefore I am." Tournier suggests a woman would say, "I relate, therefore I am." A woman's consciousness of existence is imbedded in relationships.

Tournier goes on to say that women express feelings more easily than men. A man finds it much harder than a woman to let his heart speak. Someone has said that when a man speaks, he gives you a piece of his mind. When a woman speaks, she gives you a piece of her heart. The man is much more at ease in the world of objects than the world of persons. Therefore it follows that most men are into "quantity," and most women are into "quality." Or "how many" versus "how good." A man may have many friends, but know none of them very well. A woman may not have as many friends, but it doesn't matter, because she is concerned about the depth of each relationship and how well she knows the person.

Another thing Paul Tournier talks about is women in the marketplace. When some women start working, they try to become "men" by being more concerned about getting ahead than about the people involved in their work. This makes women appear hard and aggressive. If a woman could only understand that she can be a force in the marketplace and still express her softness and concern for others, she would be so far ahead of men in general. Actually there has to be a balance for both sexes. Not just a desire for things and getting ahead in a career, and not just personal relationships; it takes a combination of both.

I have a sister-in-law who went into the fresh and silk flower business with a friend. In one month after buying the shop, they doubled the business. The reason they're such good business people is that they take care of the customers. They know their customers' names, their color preferences and other likes and dislikes, and the number of people in their family. They are not just pushing for the sale. They are also caring for the people involved.

Chuck has already mentioned our way of talking on the phone as an example of our different approach.

Some men love to talk on the phone, but most men's business conversations go something like this: "Hi, Jim. How's the old golf game? . . . Missed the birdie on three, did you? . . . Say, I need fourteen more cases of oil by Friday; can you get it here? . . . Great. Say hello to Margaret. . . . Goodbye."

On the other hand, a woman might say: "Hello, Sally, how was your weekend? . . . Oh really, was he sick the whole time? . . . Are the other kids okay? . . . Sure hope your Mom doesn't come down with it, after being there. . . . (A few more minutes of relationship talk). Well I'd better go. Oh, by the way I need fourteen more cases of oil by Friday. Any problem? . . . Good. Sure hope the kids get better. . . . Let's have lunch soon. We never seem to have enough time to talk. . . . Sounds great. Goodbye."

Even though their business conversations are not long, many times women will be the best of friends without ever having met each other in person. They will know how many children each other has, what their husbands do, where they are from, what area of the city they live in, and so on. Two men might talk on the phone weekly for years, and know very little about each other.

My guess is that a man could exist much longer on a deserted island than a woman could. He would be into getting things organized, while she would probably die quickly for lack of meaningful relationships.

Maybe that's why we've never heard of Roberta Crusoe.

4

It Was Twisp!
It Was
Winthrop!

(BARB:) We have a tennis court at our home, and right after we moved in Chuck wanted to put a cover over it. It rains a lot in the winter in Seattle, and he thought we could use it more if it was covered. Since he wanted me to let him dream without asking him about all the details, I just let him talk and dream and talk and dream. I knew there was no way we could afford the cover, and more than that, I just didn't want to ruin the feel of the woods and the peacefulness of the setting.

One day one of our clients placed a big order, and all of a sudden Chuck thought we could afford the cover. He was so excited. Then I had to say, "There is something I haven't told you. I don't *want* a cover on the tennis court; it will look like a warehouse, and won't fit in with the woods." He was amazed I hadn't said anything earlier. In fact, he thought it was funny!

(CHUCK:) I did?

Yes, you did. You laughed a lot.

That's not the way I remember it, but since I'm not into details, I'll give you the benefit of the doubt. We still don't have a cover over our tennis court. Think of all the extra exercise I would get. It would probably help me prevent a heart attack, so Barb won't have to sell the house to pay taxes and move to Skid Road. In fact I feel a little weak right now, but maybe it will pass.

Men are usually into the big picture, and women are usually more into details. When the family moves to Kansas City for the new job, the husband is going for the goal—the job. It's his wife who remembers to pick up the kids from school, sell the house, and turn out the lights. The man just wants to get going toward his goal. This can be a cause of conflict if both partners are not aware of what's happening. The man will feel threatened because he "failed" to remember the details, and the woman will be panicky because there is so much to do before they can go.

This is what happens. The man comes up with a big goal. He's all excited and all he sees is the goal. The woman can usually see how to *get* to the goal, and asks things like "What about this?" or "Have you thought about that?" But when I'd ask questions, Chuck would say, "Don't you have confidence in me?" He was just thinking about the end result and I was thinking about how he was going to get there. I'm sure men feel that we women enjoy popping their balloons because we ask about details and give them our opinions.

It does feel like you're popping our balloons. When I present a dream to Barb, she tells me all the reasons why it won't work. My problem is that I back off too soon. I need to do a better job filling her in on the details without getting defensive. I've asked her to just let me dream without adding too many details. When I reach for the phone to call the contractor, THEN she can give me her opinions.

Another way we notice that women are into details and men into goals is when we get in the car to go some place. I'll have the trip all planned in my mind as to what streets to take. Chuck just starts out. He doesn't really know how he's going to get there. He just knows he's here, and eventually wants to be there.

Chuck by habit heads the car toward work when we should be going to church. He goes north when our destination is south. He turns right out of our driveway instead of left. It's especially bad when we have friends in the car and I don't want to look like a back-seat driver, telling him what to do. Dr. Henry Brandt tells of the time he found himself going the wrong way on the freeway after declining his wife's direction advice, and then struggling to figure out a way to turn the car around without his wife noticing.

Chuck says he does pretty well when I'm not in the car, but I wonder how he makes it to work.

It used to bother me to have Barb say, "Why didn't you turn there?" or "Why are we going in this direction?" or "Shouldn't we have taken that exit back there?" Finally I realized that I WASN'T the best navigator in the family and I turned all of that over to Barb. I told her I would be writing commercials or building furniture in my mind while I was driving, and it was up to her to make sure we got to where we were going.

Women seem to have this pressing need not only to pay attention to details, but to get them RIGHT! I had no idea Barb had that need. I would be telling a story at dinner with some friends. All of a sudden Barb would interrupt with a detail I had missed or gotten wrong. (She says she thought during our early years of marriage that I was lying.) Then after adding a couple of corrections, she would take over the whole story and I sat there steaming inside. Who cares if I did get my details mixed up a bit? At least I got to the right point.

One time one of the people who worked for us asked me about the sights to see in Twisp, a small town we had visited in Eastern Washington—

It was Winthrop.

It was? Okay. Winthrop. I suggested she and her husband eat in the local hotel because all the retired men in the community had breakfast there, and it was colorful to hear them banter back and forth. When she got back from her vacation, this person told Barb how much they regretted not having had time to eat in the hotel Chuck told them about. Barb said, "What hotel?" I guess the hotel I was talking about was in a different small town—175 miles away. When you've seen one small town hotel you've seen them all. How could I remember a piddly detail like that? A hotel is a hotel.

The way I learned to handle Barb interrupting my stories was to look at ourselves as a baseball broadcast team. Dave Niehaus does the play-by-play for the Seattle Mariners, and he might be reporting that Harold Reynolds was rounding second on his way to third, and right then Rick Rizz, the color man, would INTERRUPT and say that Harold was batting .289, was leading the league in stolen bases, lived in Corvallis, Oregon, in the off season, and liked pizza. Did Dave get all threatened when Rick interrupted? Not at all. So now when Barb and I are out for dinner, I just consider myself doing the play-by-play, and Barb is adding the color because she has this strange need to get the details accurate.

Why were you so threatened when I added details?

Because it made me feel like a two-year-old to be corrected all the time. I felt like I had failed again. I couldn't even tell a story right.

But that wasn't my intent.

It wasn't?

No—we women just want to get the details straight. It has nothing to do with you. I just don't think the story is nearly as much fun when the details aren't right.

Chuck also gets two or three different events mixed up together as one story. He just can't remember. If you realize your husband really *can't* remember, and you know he really *isn't* lying, you can just let him tell his stories any old way he wants—even though he'll get into trouble by ending up at a dead end, and will wonder how he got there, and you'll have to bail him out. Now when that happens to Chuck and me, we just look at each other and laugh.

We men have to understand how much women are into details. For instance, the husband comes home from work and says, "Is dinner ready?" His wife says, "I left the office on time and stopped by the day-care center, but Cliffy wasn't anywhere to be found and they finally located him hiding in a closet, and we stopped by the supermarket on our way home to get some T-bones for tomorrow and I ran into Kathy and she told me what a horrible time they are having finding a house to buy, and then I took the wrong exit off the freeway and had to stop and get the paper, and I ran into Mrs. Rice—you know she's the one who sits way down

front on the left side at church and runs the Awanas program—which reminds me there is a church dinner this Saturday and I'll need the punch bowl up from the basement
—then I stopped to get the paper and no, dinner is not
ready." All her husband wanted to know was whether he
would have time to change his clothes or check the headlines before he had to make an appearance in the kitchen.
He really didn't need all those details.

Or the husband will come home and the wife will say,
"Notice anything different?" The husband knows instantly
he is in big trouble. "Got a new davenport—my that's
pretty!" (No, we didn't get a new davenport.) "You had the
place painted, I love the color." (No, I didn't get the place
painted. I got the drapes cleaned.) He didn't even know
they HAD drapes, let alone whether they were dirty.

Or another time she might say, "Notice anything different?" The husband says, "Got a new davenport?" No, she
has cleaned and reorganized the cupboards, and now the
cloves are next to the celery salt. Or he comes home and she
says, "Notice anything different?" He mentions the davenport and she says she got her hair done. The problem with
Barb's haircuts is that her hairstylist cuts her hair with a mi-
croscope. He goes "snippy snip here, and snippy snip
there—that will be forty dollars please." Her hair is one-bil-
lionth of a millimeter shorter and I'm supposed to notice.
Wives, don't be afraid to give your husband hints like
"Notice anything different about my hair?" and "Don't you
think the drapes look better cleaned?" He needs those hints
badly.

I think sometimes a man remembers what he
wants to. Way back in the olden days, Chuck used to
fix black-and-white TV sets to earn a little extra money.
He knew which tube handled the audio, which was
the high voltage tube, and which one controlled the
horizontal hold. He even knew the names and num-

bers by heart, but he couldn't for the life of him remember to put the plastic dishes in the *top* of the dishwasher, or remember which way Beverly's dress went
on. I went to church early one day when Bev was
small, and left her for Chuck to dress. When she got to
church she not only didn't have her dress on right
(Chuck thought buttons always went in front) but she
wasn't sliding down the slide very well because she
didn't have any panties on.

Maybe this has something to do with that brain surgery a
man gets right after the wedding ceremony.

5

A Chair Is a Chair Is a Chair

(BARB:) When we first came to Seattle in 1958 we moved into a home where we were given permission to paint the rooms and take the money off our rent. I told Chuck I wanted everything off-white. He told me he thought that was "dumb."

(CHUCK:) I didn't say it was dumb, I just couldn't imagine anyone having all the rooms off-white.

You did too say it was dumb; but we were young then and didn't know better than to say things like that to each other. Every room of the house opened onto the large, connected living and dining room. I wanted to please Chuck, so I let him pick the colors. I did get to paint all the woodwork white. But he picked a bright harvest gold for the living and dining room. One bedroom was a spring pink. Next to it was a light blue bathroom. Further down on the left was a spring blue kitchen, and at the end of the living room we looked right into another bedroom which was the brightest apple green you've ever seen.

This was before the days of "color draping," so we didn't know that my coloring is autumn. The spring colors were okay—but not all so close together.

I thought the house was beautiful—and besides, those were the colors I could get on sale. Does the White House in Washington have every room off-white? Of course not. There's the "Green Room" and the "Blue Room," and the "East Room" is gold.

Besides, I was raised on a farm where you used the paint you had on hand regardless of whether it was "right" or not. (I remember painting the seats of our halfway house, as we called it. It was halfway from our back door to the chicken house . Uncle Clarence came in from work one day and sat down on the newly painted seats. I had forgotten to put up a sign. I can still remember vividly the scene of my grandmother taking the paint off my uncle's posterior with turpentine, as he mumbled words that I probably shouldn't put in this book. He was so patient with me. I don't know how he did it.)

In our next house I made sure we painted everything off-white and used pillows and furnishings for accent colors. We just don't believe the man should be choosing the colors or furnishings for the home, because the home is the extension of his *wife's* personality, not his. The home is her work place. This is where she spends most of her time and energy, even if she works in the marketplace. This is where people will come in and comment on "her" decorating.

This also means when my home has leaky faucets or broken pipes, I don't feel right. Chuck always likes to kid me and say that when the roof gutters are plugged up, I'm plugged up.

I believe this difference in the husband's and wife's view of the home is God-designed rather than cultural, hereditary, or environmental. The reason I believe it is that God tells the man (in the book of Genesis) that he is to be the provider, and He tells the woman (in the book of Titus) to be the keeper or guardian of the home. So even if she is working, as the Proverbs 31 woman worked, she still has the feeling that if all is not right at home, *she* is not right.

When I worked for Chuck at the advertising agency, my mind was always on what had to be done at home. Did I have the ironing done? Was the wash done and put away? Did I have the right food in the cupboard so Chuck could have his can of chili or tuna fish?

I mentioned earlier the time when Chuck was buying equipment for the business rather than carpets for the house. We understood why we were disagreeing about this only after we learned this principle of the wife's priority in determining the look of things at home. When he said he was buying the equipment for "me" because it was for the business, that was true. He was providing for me. But oh, how I wanted to get my home fixed up to reflect my own taste and personality.

What we were doing—and Barb really hasn't quite gotten a full understanding of it yet—was dividing our priorities between "wants" and "needs." For instance, we NEEDED a new camera at work; we wanted a new rug. We NEEDED a new recorder; we wanted new curtains. We NEEDED a new stereo; we wanted to have the porch painted. See how that divides up? I'm not sure why Barb didn't understand that.

For years Chuck not only bought exercise and business equipment, he has also purchased countless tools. And each time he would buy another tool, he would exclaim that I just didn't know how wonderful it was to have the right tool. Then suddenly, after thirty years, I realized that the same could have been said for the things I needed in the home. I may be slow, but I'm sharp!

We have a red velvet chair in our home. We've had a number of conflicts over this particular chair, because our dog Muffit loves to sit in it tucked in alongside Chuck's leg. A *hairy* red chair did not express who I was. Chuck had a hard time understanding this, so the offense was repeated. Then he read James Dobson's book *What Wives Wish Their Husbands Knew About Women.* That was where he learned about the home being the extension of my personality. Until then he thought a chair was a chair was a chair.

Also, do you men realize that the home is the woman's work place too? And that we cannot begin our work until we have picked up everything you've left out all over the house? An illustration came to me one day as we were doing a seminar for a group of coaches and their wives. I asked the coaches how they would like to go out on the football field everyday before practice and pick up their wife's slips, bras, pantyhose and other whatnots before they could start work. Of course everyone laughed, but that is what it is like for women when the family leaves all their things around the house for us to pick up.

For years, each time we were expecting guests I would go into the bathroom to straighten and add clean towels. Then Chuck would come home from work and I would have to go into the bathroom and clean and straighten the towels *again* before the guests arrived. I asked him who he thought straightened up everything after he finished in the bathroom. It just had never occurred to him to ask, but now that he knows who does it, he carefully wipes down the sink and makes sure he hangs the towel right. I don't know why I didn't think until last year to tell him about this.

Hold it! That's not correct. I KNOW I have been doing that for years. I think Barb's having memory lapses or something.

Speaking of towels reminds me of the times we go to someone's home, and on the counter or towel racks in the bathroom are those tiny dainty towels that would hardly make a good handkerchief. You can wipe one finger at a time. When I go into a bathroom like that, I usually rummage around in the family closet and find some big towels stuffed behind boxes. I'm surely not going to soil the little bitty ones. Also I'm amazed at the type of soap women put in guest bathrooms, designed like fairies or sheep or little duckies. Who in their right mind would put water on those? Again, I just look behind the shaving cream in the medicine chest and can usually find an old sliver of Ivory to use.

Now here's another strange thing about women: Did you know that our wives' self-esteem is connected with what WE wear and how WE look? Learning this was a big shock to me. I had no idea. I knew Barb took lots of time to fuss with her own appearance, but I didn't think she cared how I looked. Yet women really do want their husbands to look presentable.

Sometimes I'll come downstairs after getting ready for work and Barb will say something like "YUCK," which translated means I have the wrong tie on, or my shirt doesn't go with my pants. I have to admit the only taste I have is in my mouth, but I used to resent it when I was made to feel I had failed again because I couldn't even DRESS right. I didn't realize that if I went out of the house looking odd, the women who see me on the street would not say, "Chuck doesn't have very good taste in clothes," but rather, "What's wrong with Barb that she doesn't catch those things?"

One way to solve this problem, men, is to have your wife go through all your clothes and assign animal labels to each piece. If you find a shirt, pair of pants, coat and tie all with an elephant on them, then you know it's safe to dress and go to work. But if you find a rhino on the tie and an elephant on the shirt, make a change. Why be the laughing-stock of the town?

Because my self-esteem is at stake, I have asked Barb not to come at me so hard when she has a suggestion about my clothes. So one day, as we were planning to go out, she said, "Won't you be cold without a sports coat?" (No, I'll be warm enough.) "Are you sure you won't be too cold without a sports coat on?" (No, I'm sure I'll be fine.) "You would LOOK better with a sports coat on" (Oh I would LOOK better—no problem, glad to wear one). I know this seems like a terrible effort, women, but believe it or not, men are quite fragile and you have to be tender with their egos.

By the way, I think men's fashions are a women's conspiracy anyway. We are so much more comfortable in our jeans and work shirts, but to please our wives we have to put on a straightjacket and choke ourselves with ties. Do you know where the custom of wearing neckties originated? I understand a queen of England once tried to hang her husband. The rope broke and he lived, but she liked the effect of the rope around his neck so much that she decreed that all men forevermore must be thus attired in public.

I think all this worry about how a husband looks may be the only real tie-in to evolution. There just isn't much evidence at all to support the theory of evolution, but maybe this could be one little shred. Does your wife ever pick little specks off your collar, or adjust your eyebrows, or straighten your tie, or pick something out of your ear? Do you like that? I don't either. But we need to be sympathetic because that might be a holdover from the time we were monkeys. Have you ever gone to the zoo and watched the female monkeys picking fleas off their sons and husbands? It's the same thing. Tell your atheist-evolutionist friends about this; they need desperately a new breakthrough.

What we men need to do is realize that since our wives' self-esteem is tied up in how we look, we shouldn't go out with a scruffy beard or dirty Levis or the wrong tie. Since your wife is your highest priority, according to the Bible, the least you can do is live in an understanding way with her and go along with the program in the personal appearance department.

By the way, Barb is careful not to make me uncomfortable in her choice of clothes for me. She may stretch my tastes once in awhile with some new fashion, but most of the time I eventually come to like it.

There was one exception. A few years ago we had a football game scheduled in Pullman with Washington State University. Since the forecast was for very cold weather and it was a night game, Barb decided to get us some Moon Boots. They looked pretty swishy and sweet, but I figured they would keep me warm, so I agreed to wear them. As usual, I was on the sidelines with the Husky team, but I felt terribly out of place because all the REAL men down there had on Adidas or Nike shoes. No one had Moon Boots— except me. I tried to pull my pants down to hide them, but that became a little drafty. I noticed the crowd begin to snicker and point to my boots. It turned out all right, however. On one of the critical plays, an opposing running back came sweeping around the end right toward me. When he saw my Moon Boots he started laughing, which slowed him down enough that our guys caught up with him and threw him for a big loss. At least I contributed something, but it still felt a little odd. Strangely, those boots have become lost. I can't find them anyplace. I've looked and looked.

While we were still learning a lot about marriage, we purchased a very large home on four wooded acres. When we moved in Chuck had goals and expected great things from me. We were not a team at that time, however, because he was making a series of investments that were failing. I had a resistant spirit, and did not want to do everything he was dreaming about, and that included all his plans for using the house. He was inviting everyone in Seattle over for meetings. His idea of a successful evening was to have 150 people over. My idea was to have a candlelight dinner for four. I just couldn't seem to make him hear where I was coming from.

Things in our marriage had been fairly even through the years, but when we moved into the big house we really found out we were two different people. I started to hate living in that house. Having a nice home means nothing if your relationship is not good. I kept trying to tell him how I felt, but he just didn't hear me.

One of the things he liked to do was have the Seahawk football team and Mariners baseball team over for a tennis-swim party each year. This particular year I was extra tired because I needed to have surgery. He wrote me a note saying I could decide whether or not to have the teams over, and as usual he said, "Don't go to any trouble. Just have it catered." But I'm just a farm girl from Wenatchee, where we always did our own cooking. Besides, I had already tried a caterer once and he put his steam trays on my oak dining room table and dripped hot water all over them. And when he poured coffee, he didn't use a napkin to stop the drips, so the cream-colored carpet was a mass of spots. I didn't want anything to do with caterers again. (Now that I've had more experience and know some wonderful people in the catering business, I've learned what a great help they can be.)

As we talked about caterers, Chuck said again that I had a resistant spirit, and as I've mentioned, I did! I

I didn't reply to his note about deciding "whether or not" to have the teams over, because I had chosen "or not." It was during this time that Chuck was having some hard times at work, and I decided to fast and pray for him. On the day I was fasting, he came home and asked me again about having the parties. It was evident I really didn't have a choice, so I said I would do it; and with my "no coffee" headache I went out to the kitchen to start baking. He saw me in the kitchen and was mad at me for doing too much!

I sound like a real beast, don't I? But I didn't mean to give Barb a bad time. I just felt God wanted us to use our large home to entertain His people. Barb wasn't against this; she wanted to use the house too. We just had different expectations. In addition to having our athlete friends over, I was visualizing sharing the facilities of this beautiful large home with people who could not afford this type of privacy and convenience. Her vision was having one or two couples over and having a quiet, intimate dinner with candlelight. We had never talked about our expectations and visions, so the resistance we felt from each other was all under the surface. We had no idea what was the matter. All I know is that I was stretching her energy level to the maximum. I really don't know how she survived those days.

As far as I was concerned, when we had a group over all we had to do was zip down to our friendly supermarket and pick up some Mother's cookies, some peanuts and an orange or two, and we were in business. That way we didn't have to do all that third-world-war baking and slaving, vacuuming and dusting. I didn't want to play games with our guests. They needed to see me just like I was— messy. Why all this fuss just to have a few hundred people over? I just couldn't understand the problem.It was almost like Barb didn't want it to appear that anyone lived in the house. If that's what she wanted, then we should just put up ropes like they do in George Washington's home, and no one would mess up anything.

Chuck had not learned yet that the home is an extension of my personality. Caterers and Mother's cookies were just not "me," and would not reflect the type of cooking and serving I wanted done. I wanted to serve our guests myself. Chuck shows love by taking people to dinner at a restaurant. I wanted to do something more personal.

As Chuck sensed my resistant spirit, he would say, "I just feel it's the Lord's will that we have this group over." I hated that! The Lord had not mentioned one word about it to me!

One time we had a dearly loved couple staying with us. They had gone out to dinner with some friends, so Chuck and I also went out to a restaurant. We had a big conflict that evening, but since we were at the restaurant we had to be discreet, even though our emotions were running high.

As we drove up to the house that night, we noticed that our friends had already returned. As we sat in the car for a minute, Chuck told me how swamped he was at work, and said he just couldn't go in and entertain. He just had to go back to work.

I had been taught the value of word pictures by Gary Smalley (who together with John Trent has written about this in their book *The Language of Love*), so I decided to try one out. I told Chuck, "How would you feel if I told you it was the Lord's will for you to come in the house and entertain? You would hate it. That's how I feel when you tell me it's God's will to do something I just don't feel I can do." Because I had pictured something with which he could relate, he understood and has never said that to me again.

I painted another word picture for him that night.

One of his favorite people at Safeway was having a retirement party the next week, and Chuck stayed up nights to work on a "This Is Your Life" presentation for him. He used slides and multiple screens with lots of humor and good background music, with everything automated. This was his way of showing love to his friend. As we were talking about using caterers, I asked him how he would feel if I asked him to have one of his helpers do the slide presentation. Even though he knew others could do a good job, it wouldn't be exactly the way he was doing it. "That's how I feel about caterers," I told him. Not once since that time has Chuck insisted on having caterers. He understood perfectly what I was feeling. The principle is to relate a problem to their world so they can identify what you're feeling.

One of my friends described herself to her husband as a daisy who was wilted and her petals were dropping off one by one. Gary Smalley uses the example of a wife who described herself as a car. Her upholstery was ripped, all her tires were flat, her paint was peeling off, there was no oil in her crankcase and her gas tank was empty. Most husbands could clearly identify with how she was feeling. This works the other way too—where a husband gives his wife word pictures—but it's usually the man who needs the picture, since he's not that gifted in observing feelings.

Before I read Dr. Dobson's book about wives and began living in a more understanding way with Barb, I thought a faucet was a faucet and a gutter was a gutter. I had no idea it was mixed up in Barb's personality or self-esteem.

I don't know if your house has rain gutters, but at our home in Seattle they keep filling up with leaves. My idea is to let them get filled up until there is no room for any more, and then the leaves will just fall to the ground. Barb's idea is to clean the gutters at least once a year. I hate cleaning gutters, and my nature is to get halfway through the job and give it up until the next time I don't have anything better to do. After I learned that Barb didn't feel good when the gutters were full, it helped me grit my teeth and finish the job even though I really didn't feel like it at the time.

Barb has this thing about leaves. She can hear each one "click" as it leaves its mother branch and flutters to the ground. Every time a leaf falls, Barb wants me to go out and rake it up. My idea of using the Lord's time wisely is to wait until February when all of the leaves have fallen, and then rake them all up at once. Who cares if we are up to our waists in leaves? They make a soft landing spot if we fall—a consideration that is becoming more important at our age because our bones are so brittle. But since Barb feels messy if there are leaves all over the place—guess what happens? We rake up the leaves.

And then there's the patio. It gets rained on quite a bit, so the green moss thrives. Barb wants me to go out there and kill all those innocent mosslings. All I can think of as I am murdering mosslings is the mossling family sitting down to dinner and everyone wondering where Grandpa mossling is. He's one of the ones Barb made me do away with. Just because they make the patio slippery and threaten the safety of our houseguests is no reason to take this drastic action. However, when I found out that Barb is green if I don't kill the moss, I went ahead with the job.

Because the leaves, gutters, faucets and mosslings never make my top twenty priority list, I have some note paper on the refrigerator where I list my goals in serving Barb. Every time I go to get something to eat, this list stares me in the face telling me about all the things that need to be done to make Barb feel better in her home.

By the way, I suggest both partners put up a goal list. We are usually so different, we would never even think about the other person's goals if we weren't reminded.

And if that fails, ladies, there are some drastic measures you can take. For instance, let's assume one of the faucets is leaking and you don't feel good when it leaks, even though it's not a big deal to lose a few hundred gallons of water when you get lots of rain. What you should do is go to the garage and get a hammer, chisel, punch, and crowbar. When you return, you tell your husband, who is reading the paper at the kitchen table, that he does not have to worry about the leaky faucet any more because you will fix it and save him the trouble. So you begin pounding on the leaky faucet with the crowbar, hammer and chisel. It won't be long before he puts down his paper, goes to the garage for the pipe wrench, screwdriver and rubber washer so he can fix the faucet "right."

Now comes the hard part. I think you can guess why he's more likely to fix the neighbor lady's faucet before yours. The neighbor lady tells him how talented and wonderful he is. When he fixes YOUR faucet, the best he can usually expect is "It's about time." So, even though you know perfectly well how to fix a faucet properly, after he completes his work with the pipe wrench and screwdriver, you have to pretend to be "amazed" that he's so talented. Praise him, honor him, lift him up—and he'll probably change ALL the faucet washers for good measure while he's at it.

6

Seriously Now

(CHUCK:) I'm sure by now you've picked up some not-too-subtle hints that we approach marriage from a biblical standpoint, and that's true. Even if you're not a Christian, we hope you'll continue with us as we share the details of our relationship. We just feel that the Bible has many practical suggestions on marriage and relationships, and they will work whether or not you know Jesus Christ personally. At the end of the book you may decide to agree-to-disagree with us, and that will make no difference as far as our respect and love for you is concerned. We're not pressing for agreement, but simply sharing some biblical principles that have changed our lives and marriage.

There is one small problem, however: If you don't know Jesus Christ personally and have the Holy Spirit living inside you, you really don't have the supernatural power in your life to change. Oh, you might be better for a couple of weeks because the principles do work, but it takes God's power to control our anger, to love when we don't feel loving, to forgive when we don't feel forgiving, to give when we feel like getting.

Also, as we take a look at what the Bible says about marriage, let me point out that Barb and I approach Scripture differently too. Neither one of us is wrong, we're just different. We even prefer different translations of the Bible, which isn't surprising, since we're the World's Most Opposite Couple. So when you see a Scripture quoted in Barb's writing, assume it comes from the *New American Standard Bible*. If you see a Scripture quoted when I'm talking to you, assume it comes from *The Living Bible*.

I guess you could say we are walking examples of 2 Corinthians 1:3-5:

What a wonderful God we have! He is the Father of our Lord Jesus Christ, the source of every mercy, and the one who so wonderfully comforts and strengthens us in our hardships and trials. And why does He do this? So that when others are troubled, needing our sympathy and encouragement, we can pass on to them this same help and comfort God has given us.

The main reason Barb and I might be able to help you with some of your marriage struggles is that we have experienced many of the same things. We've gone THROUGH the difficulties, so now we can pass on the same comfort and encouragement God gave us as we went through them.

There is one area, however, where Barb and I can't relate directly: When I went through my midlife crisis I didn't get around to my affair. I guess I was busy at the time and somehow missed it. I would have enjoyed my Porsche and my gold medallion displayed against my hairy chest, but it's too late now—so I'll have to let someone else tell you about that area. But if it's communication problems you're having and these seem to make up most marriage struggles anyway) then you've come to the right place, because we're the experts in the struggle to communicate.

It might surprise you, but differences between marriage partners are DESIGNED by God. It wasn't an accident. That was the way He set up the system. Genesis 2:18 tells us:

And the Lord God said, "It isn't good for man to be alone; I will make a companion for him, a helper suited to his needs."

The first thing in His creation that God said wasn't good was man's being alone. I'm reminded of this every time Barb goes home to visit her mom. I have all these great plans and lists of things I am going to get done while she is gone. I can work twenty-four hours a day if I want to. I don't have to eat, or I can eat nineteen meals a day. I am independent and can come and go as I like. Then she leaves. Suddenly all my plans and goals don't seem so exciting anymore, and I tend to mope around, watch too much TV, and go to bed too early. I can hardly wait for her return. All this after more than thirty years of marriage!

The word "man" used in the above Scripture probably means "mankind," because a woman can be just as alone without a man as a man is without a woman.

The Hebrew word translated "helper" in the passage suggests "completer." But for a man and woman to complete each other, they have to be different. Remember, this doesn't mean you're weird if you're more alike than different. We're just talking about the majority of husbands and wives. And even if you are more the same than different, I would be willing to bet that your God-designed male-female differences still make your relationship tense once in a while.

God has both male and female characteristics, and He divided Himself, so to speak, when he made men and women. We've been trying to get back together ever since.

This explains why a man leaves his father and mother, and is joined to his wife in such a way that the two become one person..
(Genesis 2:24)

The Hebrew word translated as "joined" refers to a very strong bond, like being "glued" to each other. That's why divorce is so destructive. It's like trying to tear apart two pieces of paper that have been glued together. You just end up ripping them. Divorce always leaves scars, whether or not the man or woman becomes a Christian afterward and finds forgiveness in Christ. We will still suffer the natural consequences of our actions. God forgives divorce like He does any other sin, as long as we sincerely ask His forgiveness with a broken spirit, agonizing over our sin as King David did in the Old Testament. David became a "man after God's own heart" because his spirit was right, but he still suffered the natural consequences of his actions.

I am bothered by the number of evangelical churches which treat divorced people as if they had leprosy. They don't feel welcome in the "marrieds" class on Sunday morning. They really don't feel comfortable in the "singles" class either. They don't fit in with the "college-career" class, especially if they are a little older. They don't belong anywhere, it seems, so they become discouraged and finally come to the conclusion no one wants them. Depression often sets in as a result.

Sin is sin. God put envy right next to murder in the list of sins described in Romans 1:29. Divorce is caused by the sins committed by one or both partners—usually both. Sins like selfishness, greed, lust and apathy abound. But we need to quickly restore divorced people to the fellowship after they have agonized over their sin, are broken before the Lord, and desire to pick up the pieces with God's help and go on with their lives. We need to help them draw a line in the sand, saying to themselves and God: "I will no longer look to the past. From this day on, I will focus on the future and the things God wants to accomplish through me." There ARE natural consequences of divorce. These go on to a certain extent throughout a lifetime, whether the people involved are Christians or not, but people don't have to keep dwelling on the negative. Since God forgives our mistakes, we can forgive others for their mistakes too, and help them go on.

If a divorced person enters a new relationship he (or she) should determine in his heart that this marriage will last the rest of his life. That's the key for any marriage—lifetime commitment. What that does is eliminate any chance of emotional blackmail. How many times do you hear about one partner saying, "If you say (or do) that again, I'm out of here." If a person is always threatening to leave, then the other partner can never really say how they feel, or bring up a subject on which there will be disagreement. A lifetime commitment allows us to have disagreements and struggles and fights without destroying the relationship. Barb read in *The Kink and I* that we are to love each other when we feel like it, when we don't feel like it, and until we feel like it. If you have not verbally made a lifetime commitment to your partner, please close this book and take care of that right now. Unless both of you have this security, everything else we say is meaningless.

(BARB:) I read a poem the other day by Ruth Harmes Calkins that portrays the pain a troubled marriage can cause. It's called "He Said...She Said":

Another marriage is shattered, Lord, the divorce will be
   final next week.
He said it was the breakdown of communication and the
   subtle infiltration of boredom.
She said it was an accumulation of things.
He said she was unnecessarily preoccupied with home, chil-
   dren and activities.
She said he stifled her dreams and ignored her achieve-
   ments.
He said he felt in prison, restricted; that night-after-night
   he got the old pushaway.

*She said he was harsh and brutal and often embarrassed her
     in public.*
*He said her critical attitude contributed to his sense of inad-
     equacy.*
*She said she felt lonely and unappreciated with no claim to
     personal identity.*
*He said she wallowed in self-pity and refused to acknowl-
     edge her benefits.*
She said he was shiftless and irresponsible.
He said she didn't understand.
She said he didn't care.
*Lord, how tragic that through all the wasted years, neither
     of them asked what YOU'VE said.*

Our purpose in this book is to tell you what the
Lord has done for us, what He has taught us concerning differences, and to teach you what the Scriptures
have to say about the marriage relationship, as well as
other relationships. We have found that so many of the
principles God gives us for marriage apply to our
friendships too.

I think Philippians 2:3-11 holds the key to getting
along with each other:

*Do nothing from selfishness or empty conceit, but with
humility of mind let each of you regard one another as more
important than himself; do not merely look out for your
own personal interests, but also for the interests of others.*

*Have this attitude in yourselves which was also in
Christ Jesus, who, although He existed in the form of God,
did not regard equality with God a thing to be grasped, but
emptied Himself, taking the form of a bond-servant, and
being made in the likeness of men. And being found in appearance as a man, He humbled Himself by becoming obedient to the point of death, even death on a cross.*

Therefore also God highly exalted Him, and bestowed

*on Him the name which is above every name, that at the
name of Jesus every knee should bow, of those who are in
heaven, and on earth, and under the earth, and that every
tongue should confess that Jesus Christ is Lord, to the glory
of God the Father.*

This passage tells us how to love each other and
how Jesus Christ loved us. Since we're told to follow
His example, here is what He did and asks us to do:

First, he emptied Himself. In other words, He
denied Himself, even while He was enjoying the benefits of His home in heaven and His position as the
Honored One. He gave up his right to self-benefit.

Second, He became a bondservant. A bondservant
is one who has been given his freedom, but has chosen
to remain with his master and serve him.

Third, He humbled Himself. He did not do what
He wanted, but what He was sent to do—to become a
man and live as a man, and go through the daily trials
of living.

Fourth, He became obedient to the point of death,
even death on a cross.

In all four of these, He gave up His rights to benefit
Himself, and He put others first. This is what we must
do in a marriage if it is to be all God intended it to be.

Circumstances have come your way—and will
continue to come, I'm sure—where you've thought,
You've got to be kidding, Lord! We won't know why we
have to do things the Lord's way, until we do them.
After obedience comes the knowledge of Christ. After
obedience, you know *why* you are to:

> Deny yourself
> Serve
> Be humble
> Be obedient

All four involve putting others before yourself. It sounds simple, but it is so hard to put into practice.

I once was asked what had changed my life the most. It didn't take me long to decide that it was when Chuck decided to become obedient. Things have never been the same since. I was the one who reaped most of the benefits from that decision, but Chuck disagrees because of what it says in Ephesians 5:28—

A man is really doing himself a favor and loving himself, when he loves his wife.

What we want to say over and over again is that it is okay to be different. And because of these differences there are going to be disagreements and conflicts. That's when we have to decide to be obedient, deny ourselves, and serve each other by humbling ourselves.

Even our spiritual gifts are different. Chuck has the primary gift of exhortation, and I have the primary gift of teaching. Chuck wants to emphasize living out the Lord's principles first, and I want to emphasize the Scriptures, to see how they prove themselves, and then live out the principles. Chuck doesn't think I get to the living fast enough, and I think he gets there too fast without first setting a foundation. And so it goes.

Instead of trying to mold each other into our own pattern, we need to accept and appreciate and even thank God for the differences He has designed each partner to complete the other. Jesus' instructions in Matthew 7:1-5 shows what our focus should be in relationships, and especially in marriage:

Don't criticize and then you won't be criticized. For others will treat you as you treat them. And why worry about a speck in the eye of your brother (husband/wife) when you have a board in

*your own? Should you say, "Friend, let me help you get that
speck out of your eye," when you can't even see because of the
board in your own? Hypocrite! First get rid of the board, then
you can see to help your brother.*

It's interesting to note that the original language indicates that the speck and the board are made out of the same material. This supports the idea that we tend to sense our own weaknesses in others. If we have a pride problem, we immediately spot the egotist. If we have a sensual problem, we are aware of the sexual vibrations another person gives off. If we're lazy, we get irritated when someone doesn't carry his load.

I also like the fact that God chose eye surgery as His example, because the eye is the most tender part of our body. If a person gets something in his eye and it takes medical treatment to get it out, I'm told that the doctor clamps the person's head in a viselike arrangement, then carefully and tenderly lifts the particle out. That's a beautiful picture of how we are to take specks out of other people's eyes—carefully and tenderly.

There ARE times when God asks you and I to help each other with our blind spots, but (at least in my experience) these times are quite rare. God seems to be more excited when I pay attention to my own weaknesses rather than dwelling on other people's shortcomings—especially Barb's. Rather than worrying about her weaknesses, I'm much better off taking advantage of her strengths.

Why not take time today or tonight to sit down with your partner and list all your differences? Think about them for a few days and make sure your list is as complete as possible. Then have a meeting with the Lord to present your lists to Him, thanking Him for making your mate different so he or she can be a completer to you—adding strengths you don't have.

When you CELEBRATE the differences, your marriage

will take on a whole new meaning. Conflicts over differences will begin to fade away as you accept each other right where you are.

7

Men Make the Final Decisions, Right?

(CHUCK:) I got off Barb's team in the twenty-second year of our marriage. I didn't mean to do that; in fact, I thought I was doing just the opposite. I had turned over my life to Jesus Christ one-hundred percent after attending a Bill Gothard "Basic Youth Conflicts" seminar in 1971. That one-hundred percent included my time, talents, material things, bank accounts, tennis ball machine, and everything else I owned, plus our business that we purchased that same year. Because God now owned my business, He could trust me with a little surplus. He knew we would be giving a portion of it away to His people and ministries, so He began blessing our business materially.

My method of business is to stay small, do personal service for my clients, and do much of the work myself. That way I can keep my overhead low, and do the work less expensively but just as good as anyone else in town. Our business plan is to ask God to bring in more than we give away.

If He wants to bring in less, we give away less. If He takes us to zero, then we'll sell our home and just play tennis the rest of our life. In this way God can dictate exactly what He wants us to do through the business. He is in control, and I like that.

After God began giving us a surplus, I thought we should be good stewards and put the money into some investments until God brought along the people and projects He wanted us to support. I had attended churches where I got the impression that being poor was more spiritual than having a surplus. During the first years of our marriage, I had not yet given God complete control of my life, so He was not able to bless us as much. He had promised to meet our needs, and He surely did that. We never missed a meal, and paid our bills on time, but it seemed like every time we saved a few dollars the kids would need new shoes or a tire would blow out. This seemed to reinforce the idea that God would meet our needs, but He wasn't into giving us extra. At that time I really wasn't into the Scriptures so I couldn't check that idea out, but after my life changed I ran headfirst into 2 Corinthians 9:7-8:

Everyone must make up his own mind as to how much he should give. Don't force anyone to give more than he really wants to, for cheerful givers are the ones God prizes. God is able to make it up to you by giving you everything you need and more, so that there will not only be enough for your own needs, but plenty left over to give joyfully to others.

So, according to this, God will not only meet our needs, He may give us a SURPLUS so we can give it away. And the more we give away, the more He will give us to give away. We won't be able to get ahead of Him, and we can do our giving with hilarity, as the original Greek text suggests.

I never had a surplus of money before, but now there was some left over, so I began taking my world-changing investment plans to Barb to help us be good stewards of

God's money. When I presented her with an amazing, wonderful plan, Barb would say a strange thing: "I don't FEEL good about the project." I couldn't believe it. FEEL? What does FEEL have to do with anything? How can we make sound business decisions on feelings? Look at these numbers; they fit, don't they? After some tears Barb would release me to go ahead with the investment if I felt it was God's will for our money, though she still didn't feel good about it. And since I had not yet learned that leadership means serving—not decision making—like an idiot I went ahead with the plan. Guess what? I lost the money.

The next time I took a world-changing plan to Barb, she said another very strange thing: "I don't trust those people." TRUST? You just met them at dinner the other night, but I've worked with these people for a couple of years. You don't trust them? She didn't—but said that if I thought that's what God would have us do, she wouldn't stand in the way. And again I lost the money.

There were six or seven different projects I took to her during this time, and I lost money on every one. One was to cosign a note at the bank for a divorcee who couldn't get credit. (I wasn't into Proverbs yet, where it says cosigning notes is stupid!) I remember so well this person saying she would NEVER allow me to get hurt; but one day the bank called me to pay for "my" car. She had defaulted, and I have never heard from her again.

I once wanted to sponsor a rock band that included a few members who professed to be Christians. I won't go into all the details, but I lost a great deal of money on that one. Barb didn't "feel good" about the project nor "trust" the people involved. I knew this, but I still gave them money, even some behind her back. I didn't do this to hurt her. I wasn't a beast. I loved her. I just thought God had some things for us to do and Barb never seemed to be on the same page of the program with me. I haven't had one dime of these investments returned, and don't even know where the people are now. (I wonder how such people can face themselves in the mirror in the morning knowing they have not even tried to pay their debts.)

One of my world-changing projects was to multiply the Lord's money overnight with a speculative land deal in Nevada. All I had to do was give this person money and their contact would resell the land and I would make a killing for the Lord. (Again, had I been into Proverbs I would have read that get-rich-quick schemes are also stupid). Barb suggested a very impractical thing. "Why don't you go look at the land?" Why should I look at the land? I trust the people involved. I gave them the money and THEN went down to look at the land. I now own a piece of property in the middle of Nevada somewhere. It's just sagebrush. There's nothing there, and I haven't heard from the people since.

I was going out of my mind. Here I had dedicated my resources to the Lord. I thought the projects had spiritual overtones, and yet they were blowing up in my face—every one of them. I lost thousands and thousands of dollars of the Lord's money. What was God trying to teach me? Was he really paying attention? My life's goal was to be in the center of His will. He owned everything I had, and yet things were crumbling around me, including my marriage, since I was hurting Barb at every turn by not including her in these decisions and projects. What I hadn't noticed was that she's ninety-five percent RIGHT about who to trust, and her feelings are just as reliable when it comes to relationships. By this time I was just teed off at God, and I wanted to take my dog Muffit (the only one who gave me unconditional love) and move to Maine, buy a farm, and forget people.

After one disaster the Lord and I were having one of our board meetings in the car where I was trying to figure out what He was doing to me. I was screaming at Him, questioning His judgment, asking whether He really cared.

I said, "Considering eternity past and eternity future, would you admit that you blew it once? Just once in all that time—that's not a bad record. Only once in all eternity—and that mistake was designing Barb in such a way that she disagrees with all the projects I want to get done for You."

He did not zap me with lightning or reduce me to ashes, and if I could have seen His face He might have been smiling. I got the impression that He said something like, "Remember when I opened the Red Sea for the Jewish guys and gals when Pharaoh was chasing them in the desert?" (Yes.) "Have you noticed the sun and moon I hung for you to give you warmth and light?" (I have.) "Have you noticed My design in nature—the stars, trees, animals, the marvelous way your body is designed?" (Yes.) "Then what you're really saying to Me is that Barb's heart is much too big for Me to change. In other words, even though I could hang the moon, I couldn't soften her heart toward a project I wanted you to do as a marriage team." So I confessed that yes, I guess that's really what I was saying.

Then I said to the Lord, "Okay for you! I'm not going to do ONE more thing unless Barb is in agreement. In fact, I probably won't do it even if she's just neutral." Actually, I gave up all my expectations of ever doing another project in my life. It seemed Barb had been against just about everything I wanted to do, especially in the area of investments. I assumed that since I made that vow to the Lord, Barb would now have the last word, and I would just play tennis the rest of my days. I told the Lord, "If something does come up that You want us to do, just wait until I'm through with my doubles match, and speak to me through Barb."

I was still a planner and dreamer and I still mentioned world-changing ideas to Barb. But now as I talked to her I began adding strange questions like, "How do you FEEL about this?" and "Do you TRUST these people?" Then a funny thing happened: She began to be less resistant to some of the things I felt God wanted us to do. In fact, she was even FOR some of the things I wanted to do, if you can imagine that. God was trying to teach me about marriage and about the gifts Barb had brought to our relationship.

Right about here the men to whom I tell this story are getting nervous. They're saying, "What if Barb is wrong? Eve blew it. Sarah got Abraham in trouble. What happens when your wife is against something God REALLY wants you to do?" My sincere reply is this: That's GOD'S problem. He hung the moon, and He surely can change Barb's heart if it is something He really wants us to do as a marriage team. If we miss doing something God wants us to do, God will be responsible if He doesn't make it clear through Barb. I'm through making independent decisions and harming our marriage team.

That doesn't mean she's always right; but as I've said, her track record is about ninety-five percent right when it involves relationships, and very few things in life DON'T involve relationships.

Looking back on my "Red Sea" experience as I call it, I see that this was probably the key to restoring our relationship to what it had been before, and to my getting back on Barb's team. Now I thank God for her ability to "feel" and her sensitivity in trusting—things that complete me so beautifully, but which I once resented. I wonder how I could have been so stupid. I guess I had to put Barb through all that so we could relate to where others are living.

It's so great now to make decisions together. At least most of the time it's great. There still are occasions when I grieve that Barb doesn't see the value of my latest idea. Being a team, however, releases so much of the tension, and it gives us both security. Now if we lose money by giving a loan to someone who doesn't pay it back, or through an investment in which we both were conned, it's still a learning experience but we can actually LAUGH about it. The tension is gone. We hate to lose the money, but we know we have asked for God's guidance in the matter, and we know we were united in doing what we did, so God must have something to work out in our lives through losing the money. Did you hear that? We can LAUGH about something that, before I got back on Barb's team, would have been a matter for gut-wrenching tears and conflict.

One of our best friends just lost a lot of money in the stock market because he didn't heed the warning of his wife, who didn't "feel" good about the investment. We recently met a man at one of our seminars who lost a motel chain because he didn't listen to his wife. Another man lost money in a newspaper venture because he didn't heed his wife's advice. Another man put his family through bankruptcy because he didn't take into account his wife's feelings and wisdom about his investments. Probably every person reading these words knows of some man who has disregarded the counsel of his wife, and has caused his family to suffer because of it.

Now's the time to make a verbal commitment to your wife about these kinds of matters saying you will not do a single thing unless she agrees to it. Get back on her team! Seek her counsel, listen to her feelings and trust—and then you can LAUGH with us whenever some investment or decision costs you money—after all, God owns it anyway, right?

A few years ago, the corporate headquarters of one of my clients took away a large chunk of our work. I had to let some people go, put off some equipment purchases, and tighten our belts. I was wondering whether this was the start of God taking us down to zero as far as the business was concerned, and putting us into something else. We can't give away what we don't have. Evidently God was just checking out our faith, because after He was satisfied that He still owned the place, he gave us a couple of more states to our market territory for this particular client. I guess He wasn't through with our business yet.

(BARB:) During the time Chuck was making all these financial decisions without me, we would talk and cry and then talk and cry some more. Chuck would often say, "I just don't understand it. I feel I am getting a message from the Lord to do these things. I want to do the Lord's will. Why are we having all this trouble between us? Who am I hearing from?" Neither of us had an answer at the time. I was afraid to resist too much, because I had been taught that a wife must be submissive. So I would say, "If you really think this is from the Lord, go ahead and do it." But my heart would really be screaming, "Don't do it!" I just knew it wasn't right. But I still didn't have a good reason why it wasn't right. I just knew it wasn't.

This was a time in our lives when I used to say that God and Chuck were doing things without me. Previously we had always made financial decisions together, and if one of us did not agree, we didn't do it. I knew we weren't a team anymore. It was a very hard time for both of us.

During this time Chuck was counseling with a couple who said they were Christians, but were living together without being married. At one time I thought I saw growth in their lives, so we agreed to help them out financially. Then as time went on they continued to live together, and since I saw no obedience in their lives, I thought we should no longer help them.

We had arranged our finances so that we put all income into one account. Then each month we would take a certain amount out for each of us to put into a personal account. We were not accountable to each other for this money. I could use mine to buy a special blouse or skirt, and Chuck could use his to buy tools or go golfing. But I assumed we would never buy anything we knew the other person was against.

I guess I took this arrangement between Barb and me too literally. I thought if we were not accountable to each other, then I should be able to use the money for anything I wanted, including giving it away. But this principle doesn't really work if either of the partners can have a say in how it is spent. Barb's point, however, is that I was doing something which I knew she didn't approve of. Usually the things we use our personal accounts for are more innocent.

I was looking for our family checkbook one day and accidentally opened Chuck's personal checkbook. I found entries that indicated he was still giving money to this couple behind my back. I talked to him about this and told him I would never give money to anyone that he did not want me to. He said he couldn't imagine a time when he would stop me from giving away money. (He has the gift of giving, so that is probably true.) I told him I did not think that was the point of our discussion.

And then it hit me! Would God do anything to break up our team? Would God tell us to do something that would drive us apart? No, He wouldn't. Therefore I reasoned that God would not tell either one of us to do something that the other was against, and break up the team. That answered the question as to who was telling Chuck to give money away for projects I was against, or didn't know about.

We were having a very heated discussion over the matter when the phone rang. It was a good friend to whom we both enjoyed talking. We talked, of course, like nothing was wrong. I assumed that since we had been interrupted in our discussion we would probably not talk about this again for a long time, because Chuck hated conflict so much. Chuck had taken the telephone extension at the opposite end of the house. After we hung up, I walked down the hall toward

Chuck and there he was with his arms open wide saying, "I want to be on your team."

Now I've panicked a lot of dreamers like me out there in bookland because they are married to very conservative, cautious partners who shudder when you bring up a new project. This is not a man-woman variation as much as it is a personality difference. The woman can be the dreamer and the one who rushes off into the unknown. The same principles apply to her, even if for a different reason. If her husband doesn't agree or feel good about the project, SHE should not go ahead of him.

One of the ways we dreamers fail our more conservative mates is by thinking about a world-changing plan for two weeks, then presenting it to them at dinner sometime and expecting them to get up and run around the table in glee praising our wonderful plan. More often their eyebrows twitch, they get terribly silent and maybe sweat more than usual. Then we react to their "lack of confidence" and dump our plans in the trash heap without giving our partner much of a chance to learn why we are so excited about them.

What I've done to help in this area is to write Barb notes when I first start thinking of a project or plan. This way she has the same time to think about it as I do, and when we come together at dinner she can talk objectively about it. This also eliminates body language which I tend to read the wrong way.

Now let me emphasize it again: This doesn't mean Barb is in absolute control of the family and I am just running around doing what she wants done and feeling defeated just because she is not as much of a dreamer as I am. I sincerely believe that if it is something God wants us to do, He is perfectly capable of changing and softening her heart toward the project. Biblically, I see no other alternative. In practice it works out great. As I serve her in this way, she looks to me for leadership.

8

Hi, Mom!

(BARB:) Since we've been talking about how we make decisions together, let me ask you a question: Who do you think commands the most respect in the family, or who has the most authority? Who do the football players say "Hi" to on TV? That's right—it's Mom. But why?

You've probably guessed the reason. We know Mom cooks and cleans. She gets up at night with us when we are sick, and takes us to the doctor. She shops for us, acts as our taxi driver, goes to all our sporting events, and helps at school parties. She plans meals for special occasions like birthdays, and pays attention to our likes and dislikes. In short, what gives Mom her authority in the family is the fact that she *serves.*

Here's one of our premises in this book: Headship is not decision making, but rather serving. Take a look at some Scriptures with us and see if you agree.

"You know that the rulers of the Gentiles lord it over them, and their great men exercise authority over them. It is not so among you, but whoever wishes to become great among you shall be your servant, and whoever wishes to be first among you shall be your slave, just as the Son of Man did not come to be served, but to serve and to give His life a ransom for many". (Matthew 20:25-28)

And sitting down, He called the twelve and said to them, "If anyone wants to be first, he shall be last of all, and servant of all." (Mark 9:35)

"Whoever wishes to become great among you shall be your servant; and whoever wishes to be first among you shall be slave of all. For even the Son of Man did not come to be served, but to serve, and to give His life a ransom for many." (Mark 10:43-45)

"Let him who is the greatest among you become as the youngest, and the leader as the servant. For who is greater, the one who reclines at table, or the one who serves? Is it not the one who reclines at table? But I am among you as the one who serves." (Luke 22:26-27)

We can see from these verses that God does not want us to lord it over others, but to serve one another. If our ambition is to be a leader, we should serve. Jesus Christ told us to follow His example. The word "example" means an exact tracing. We are to do as He did. He did not come to be served, but to serve, even though He was greater than those He served.

Both the Old and New Testaments make it plain we are to serve each other, but many couples fail to see how fully that's true for both the husband and wife in a marriage.

Some people who believe men are superior to women, as they point out God's words to Eve in Genesis 3:16, "And he (the man) shall rule over you (the woman)." Let me ask you a question. How does the Lord rule? He rules lovingly. He is patient. While we were yet sinners He died for us, and gave Himself up for us. He serves us. The Hebrew word for "rule" is also the word used to describe the Messiah ruling over Israel. When a husband thinks of ruling, he may think of wielding a rod of iron; but the Lord Jesus Christ rules with a scepter of love.

I would like to say it one more time: God tells us in Scripture to serve one another. The roles He gives us as men and women are given so we can best serve our mates in the way they need to be served and to feel loved. But I know some people are afraid to serve because they are afraid they will be taken advantage of. Here's what God says about that:

All of you clothe yourselves with humility toward one another, for God is opposed to the proud, but gives grace to the humble. Humble yourselves, therefore, under the mighty hand of God, that He may exalt you at the proper time, casting all your anxiety upon Him, because He cares for you. (1 Peter 5:5-7)

Here's that word "humble" again. We've talked about denying ourselves, becoming a servant, humbling ourselves and becoming obedient to the point of death. God would not ask you to do anything that is not for your good. He says to cast your care and anxiety on Him, because He cares for you. Try it His way. It works!

There is a story in 1 Kings 12 about Solomon's son Rehoboam, who had become king. His rival Jeroboam came to him one day to tell him that if he would take away the heavy yoke that Solomon had put on the people, he and his followers would serve him. Rehoboam told him to go away so he could consult the

elders who had served his father Solomon, and ask for
counsel as to how to answer Jeroboam. The elders told
him, "If you will be a servant to this people today,
grant them their petition, and speak good words to
them, then they will be your servants forever."

But he didn't listen to the counsel of the elders and
consulted instead with the young men with whom he
had grown up; they had served him. The young men
told Rehoboam to make the people's yoke even heav-
ier than what Solomon had done. And because of Rehoboam's decision to be served rather than serve, his
rival Jeroboam split the country, thereby creating separate northern and southern kingdoms.

I believe this is the reason so many marriages end
in divorce. When partners decide to serve themselves
instead of their mate, they set up a situation ripe for
conflict. This is not God's way of doing things.

Sociologist and author Tony Campolo points out
the difference between power and authority. Power is
taken, authority is earned or conferred. Therefore, as a
husband serves, the wife looks to him as her authority.
He gets what he wanted in the first place—but not by
force or deciding on his own to take it, or by being
overbearing, but by serving. The Lord tells us that
when we lose our life for another, then we'll find it.
Chuck has been my greatest example of how a husband should serve. Whenever he sees a principle in
Scripture, he obeys. I'm so grateful for him.

So we've seen that headship is not decision
making, but rather serving. It is thinking more highly
of others than we think of ourselves. It brings us back
to Philippians 2:3 again:

Do nothing from selfishness or empty conceit, but with hu-
mility of mind let each of you regard one another as more
important than himself

(CHUCK:) I'm not sure just where I got the idea that if a couple cannot agree on something, the man is to make the final decision. I think it came from something I learned at church, actually. It's so common to equate headship and leadership with decision making. And besides, it's hard taking our wives' counsel.What does she know about advertising, banking, finances, construction, mechanics or whatever the husband does for a living? It is very easy for the husband to get the mistaken idea that he should make all the final decisions around the house if the two partners can't agree. After all, the Bible says the man is supposed to be the leader, right? And that means he should make all the final decisions, right? If it comes to an impasse between the partners, then he casts the tie-breaking vote, right?

Nothing could be further from biblical truth, in our opinion. The tragedy is, many evangelical churches are teaching this type of thing. How arrogant to have one of the partners on a fifty-fifty team making independent decisions. No one would stand for that in the business world.

Jesus Christ is our example of leadership. The Bible makes it clear that Christ's headship and leadership in the Church meant he SERVED—just as a husband is to serve his wife instead of ruling with an iron fist. If one of the partners doesn't feel good about a decision, or even if one is just neutral, I would not go ahead and do it. It's simple, yet hundreds of thousands of homes are being torn apart by an indifferent, insensitive man who thinks leadership is ruling rather than serving. He is not taking advantage of the completion principle even though his wife is usually the expert when it comes to details, intuition, and relationships. A wife is fifty percent of the marriage team. She owns fifty percent of the bank account. She has a fifty percent say in how the money is spent, where the family lives, what the family does. Both husband and wife gave up the liberty to make independent decisions when they got married. In 1 Peter 3:7 we find this:

You husbands must be careful of your wives, being thoughtful of their needs and honoring them as the weaker sex. Remember that you and your wife are PARTNERS in receiving God's blessing, and if you don't treat her as you should, your prayers will not get ready answers.

And by the way, the term "weaker sex" means physically weaker—not mentally, emotionally, or spiritually. A woman isn't designed to have bulging muscles, and play contact sports against men, no matter what our culture says. I'm seeing more and more magazine ads with ladies pumping iron. I've even heard of plans for a TV show featuring women weight lifters. I guess it's okay if that's what you're into, but I prefer the women with whom I associate to be feminine, not muscle-bound. This may be one of the things that confuses me most about the women's movement. They are making such a big deal about being independent, being unique as women, being on their own, having their own strengths, able to run their own lives. Then why do they want to be like men? Beats me.

What we're saying is an extremely hard message for men. Somehow we have been taught all our lives that headship and rulership means decision making. What a shock to find out it means being a servant to our wives and often doing something THEIR way instead of our way. In other words, giving ourselves up.

Of course we are challenged on this view once in awhile, and all we can say is we hope you'll be like the Bereans. When the apostle Paul came to town, they checked the Scriptures against what he was saying. We suggest you do the same. If you don't agree with this, take another look at the Scriptures we have presented. Men are to be Christ to their wives. That means we are to have His characteristics, or at least try to. He gave up His rights. Isn't that a picture of what we should do, too?

Once in a while at one of our seminars, a man will come

up afterward and admit that he and his wife should make decisions together; then he adds, "But on the IMPORTANT ones, I should make the decision, right?" Wrong! What could be more arrogant than for one partner in a fifty-fifty team to go ahead and make independent decisions?

Men, take back your wives as partners. Work together in the decision-making process. If you can't agree on something, don't do it. If it's something God wants you to do as a team, He is plenty big enough to change one of your hearts.

9

The Attacker Gets Punished

(BARB:) Remember the expression "Opposites attract"? But the "opposite-ness" that in the beginning most attracts you about your mate later becomes your greatest irritation. He or she is just *not like you.*

When it comes to communicating, Chuck and I are nothing alike. Each of us represents one of the two different kinds of communicators God has created: the expressive and the nonexpressive. This has nothing to do with regular conversation, but it has a lot to do with how we handle conflict. Usually the nonexpressive person will want to walk away from conflict, while the expressive wants to talk about it, find out what's wrong, and be friends again. Nonexpressives do not want to talk about it, and believe that if they don't, it will go away. They feel if they just let it alone, everyone will remain friends.

Expressive people know right away why they feel

the way they do, while nonexpressives usually have no idea why they feel a certain way. All they know is that they're angry. They may even try to hide it. But it's never good to pretend you are not angry and to stuff your feelings. The trouble with stuffing is that the feelings are stuffed alive, not dead. They sit down there in a warm dark place fermenting, and pretty soon you have an explosion. On the other hand, to let your anger out in a way that hurts others, like expressive people often do, is not good either.

As you may have guessed, Chuck is the nonexpressive and I am the expressive. A friend of ours taught us a word picture that describes how we once communicated. In tennis, the ball has to go back and forth over the net in order to have a game. It's the same thing with communication. Words have to go back and forth for you to have a conversation. So often when Chuck and I had something between us that I felt needed to be examined and resolved, I would send a ball (a sentence) over the net to Chuck, and nothing would come back. I would send over another ball and it wouldn't come back. Then another and another. Pretty soon I would be slamming them over as fast as I could. Finally (as Chuck describes it), he would feebly stick out his racket and gently hit one back (a tentative expression of his feelings)—and I would either run up to the net and smash it right down his throat, or else "half-volley" it, which means not letting it get a good, high bounce before returning it.

(CHUCK:) Let me say something on behalf of all the nonexpressives out there in bookland. You see, as a nonexpressive person I need a little time to get in touch with my feelings. I'm not really sure why I'm angry or irritable or quiet.

Half of you reading this book know EXACTLY what I'm talking about. The other half can't imagine anyone not knowing what they feel at any given moment and why.

When Barb first sent all her words over the net at me, I let them go because I wasn't ready to talk just then. I might have had three or four things to say about how I felt, but when I presented point number one (that first feeble return), her immediate verbal evaluation of it was like the smash down my throat. After that, do you think I was going to mention points two, three and four? No way. Why subject myself to that type of abuse? I just got quiet, hoping the problem would go away, and gave in to keep the peace.

What I wanted was to have my tennis shots (my words) bounce nice and high (getting all my feelings out) before she tried to return them. Then I wouldn't feel so threatened and she could evaluate what I had expressed and add or question anything she wanted. I'm less verbally skilled than Barb (as so many men are in comparison to their wives), so I cannot go toe-to-toe with her in a full-blown debate and come out anything less than emotionally shattered.

> For eleven years Chuck would not tell me I was doing anything wrong. When we had a conflict, he would just get silent and say it was his problem, and I believed him. Knowing what I know now, I should have kept questioning him, but I took him at his word. I didn't know anything about "playing games"— saying one thing and thinking another. I really believed he had his own little problem, and he would be better later. I was too naive to realize that I was his little problem! If he had just talked to me about how he felt, I would have done anything for him. As it was, I thought I was the most perfect wife ever to walk the face of the earth. Even though he didn't mislead me intentionally, it really wasn't fair. If I didn't know how he felt, I couldn't do anything to help the situation. He must be superhuman to have lasted that long.
>
> My first clue that something was wrong came one evening when we were having dessert with some

friends. I guess I interrupted him for the last time he could possibly stand it, and he showed his anger in front of our friends. He didn't get mad out loud, because that's not his way. He just pulled his neck up in a certain way, and did something with his lips so I knew by his body language that something was wrong. He also got silent and did not enter into the conversation anymore. Of course I thought everyone had noticed, and we had made a pledge never to show anger to each other in public. Now here he was, angry at me for everyone to see, and he didn't even get angry with me at home.

I really don't think anyone noticed I was angry—oh maybe the women did, since they pick up on things like that. But I thought I covered myself pretty well. Part of this came from my childhood where I got the idea somehow that anger was wrong, and so I didn't express it. I just held it in. In Barb's family, they talked loud and got angry but were friends again quickly.

When I started studying anger in the Scriptures, my research showed me that God got angry for three whole pages of Strong's Concordance. Christ got angry too. He didn't just saunter into the Temple and ask the buyers and sellers to leave at their convenience—he THREW them out on their cash registers. Now if God and Christ get angry, then it's obvious that anger is not a sin—it's what we do with it that causes the problem. I've had to learn to express my anger in constructive ways, but for me it's not an easy thing to do.

Even though I'm the expressive one and Chuck the nonexpressive in our marriage, sometimes I don't have the energy to verbally work out a problem either. Once we were on our way to see the Mariners baseball team in spring training, and I got into the car and told

Chuck I had turned on our home's security alarm with the red light showing, and now I wondered if it would go off. "Yes it will," he replied and jumped out of the car to catch it before it called the police. I sat there for a while and then decided to go in and help him, but I didn't have my keys, so I rang the doorbell. Chuck says I rang it with a bad attitude.

I was on hold with the alarm company; I couldn't get the system to quit asking the police to come, and now the doorbell begins to ring. Not with a ding-dong, but with a *DING DONG DONG*. Earlier that morning I had cut myself shaving, and then my audio recorder hadn't worked properly as I was recording some commercials. Now here I was with the house coming down around my ears, and Barb was *DING-DONGING* the doorbell. Well, I lost it, I'm afraid, and became angry and aggressive and blustered.

I had been stuffing some things, if you can believe it, and I took all of Chuck's blustering very personally. We didn't have a wonderful weekend, to say the least. We were polite to each other, but we both were still angry and the fun was gone.

When Chuck and I are having a conflict, I usually pursue and Chuck withdraws. Each of us perceives something that the other does not intend. Chuck used to say about my verbal responses, "Remember when you attacked me, stuck the knife in, and blood dripped down my shirt?" How could I ever do anything that reminded him of that? It was beyond me how he could even think such a thing. Then I was startled to see in Norman Wright's book *The Christian's Use of Emotional Power* a page that had nothing else on it except the phrase, "To Disagree Is Not to Attack." Finally I understood Chuck's perception of being attacked. And I thought, *No wonder he never wants to discuss anything.*

We once heard a saying that fits here: When a man gives his opinion, a woman takes it as an opinion; but when a woman gives her opinion, the man takes it as a command. This might explain why husbands so often don't like to discuss things with their wives.

Talk about misperceptions! When I was unable to be expressive during a conflict, Barb felt I was punishing her by my silence. Later, when we were giving each other our opinions, she would say, "If I let you know how I feel, will you punish me?" I love her; I wasn't trying to punish her. And she loves me, and wasn't trying to attack me. It was just our immediate, emotional perception of the situation during the conflict.

When I came to understand how Chuck felt, I tried to back off and come at him softer. I think it was part of letting his tennis shots bounce and come up real high (getting all his feelings out) before I hit it back. Chuck wanted me to think about what he'd said for a while before I responded. But in that kind of situation two seconds seems like an eternity to me. It's so hard for me to keep quiet.

When Chuck understood that I felt punished when he withdrew, he did his best not to do that anymore. He's chosen to talk to me no matter how hard it is for him, especially when he knows our conversation could end up in a conflict or at least a difference of opinion.

And for sure it's a matter of choice. I never feel like sticking around for a conflict. There is compromise on both sides. The expressive person needs to give the nonexpressive some time to think about the problem, and the nonexpressive needs to make a date to talk about it, by saying something like, "I'll probably know better why I'm angry at breakfast. Could we wait until then to talk about it?" Or,

"Let's go out to dinner tomorrow night. I'm sure by then I can figure out what's eating at me."

I've made Barb a set of cue cards to use in a conflict situation. They have very strange sounding words on them, sentences that do not occur to Barb when we are having a heated discussion. Here are three of the sentences:

TELL ME MORE ABOUT THAT.
WHAT ELSE DO YOU FEEL?
MY, THAT'S INTERESTING.

You nonexpressives have probably never heard those words from your more expressive mate.

The "banana" principle is something that helps my expressive friends deal with us nonexpressives. When you get into a conflict with your nonexpressive partner, stick a banana in your mouth so you can't talk. Works great. Try it!

Often the nonexpressive will feel that the expressive person is nagging about something. The expressive is just trying to talk, but the nonexpressive imputes something negative, and subconsciously wants to avoid the discomfort of talking. The expressive goes ahead and brings up something that needs to be talked about and resolved, and the nonexpressive then feels like a failure.

By the way, have you ever noticed that men are not usually accused of nagging? Even the Bible speaks of the "quarrelsome" or "contentious" wife who is "like a constant dripping." I've chosen a better word that fits what men do—"badgering." They talk about something over and over and over again until you agree to do it, even though you may have doubts about it.

We spoke recently to a Sunday School class and mentioned to them the principle of not making decisions unless both partners agreed. Afterward a young couple came up and the woman was crying. It seemed

her husband had always gone on the theory that they
made decisions together, but when she did not agree,
he would keep at her and keep at her until she said she
agreed—even though she really didn't. She had been
badgered!

Chuck has used badgering when he wanted me to
agree with some goal or idea he had. He just wouldn't
quit talking about it.

Hold it! I need to explain that I'm in a no-win situation on
this. Barb has asked me not to surprise her with my goals
and ideas, so I've begun to write notes, as I mentioned earlier. Now my only problem is getting the notes back with
Barb's written comments. Barb hates to make decisions and
is uncomfortable getting involved in my world-changing
plans. So she doesn't send back my notes, hoping I will
forget about the latest big idea. However, I've decided that
if I don't get my notes back with her comments, I should
just assume that she is FOR the project.

Instead of joining her husband in a lifetime quest for
great new ideas and projects, I'm pretty sure Barb had
dreams of marrying someone who would sit on the porch
and swing with her the rest of her days. I honor that. I take
ten to fifteen minutes off every summer to swing with her.
But how could I quit talking about new ideas when they
can benefit the world so much?

I work so hard to get Chuck to finally talk, and
then when he does, I evaluate everything he says. Like,
"How could you possibly think that?" or "You're
wrong!" or some other choice little tidbit. Of course,
this closes him right back up again. I have had to learn
to be a better listener.

Our daughter Bev has taught me a lot about listening. I thought I was listening to her, but she didn't
think so. When I asked her how I could show it more,

she said I could ask her questions about what she was talking about. I think that is a real key because it lets the other person know that you have heard him and are interested in what he is saying. Sometimes I'm guilty of thinking about what I'm going to add to the conversation, rather than focusing on the other person's words and feelings.

Since our emotions run high during times of conflict, it's still hard for me to put this into practice. I still want to jump in with both feet and have my say—as I did once this morning.

I thought it was last night.

Probably both! But at least it wasn't in the car on our way to teach a seminar in communication—that's usually when we have our worst communication difficulties. You see, though we've had some successes in this area it doesn't mean we no longer have problems. We still have our unique temperaments and personalities, and it takes lots of work and commitment to go *through* the process of learning to communicate —rather than just walking away, as so many couples are doing these days.

We have what we call the "Biscuit Story" that illustrates Chuck's need to have some time to think things over before he can talk about them. When I worked with Chuck at the office he would call across the hall and ask me what we were doing for dinner. Sometimes I would say I had something in the crock pot. He would say, "Oh, you don't want to cook, let's go out for dinner." Since I was usually tired, I would welcome the opportunity to have dinner out, and when I got home I'd put the food away for another day.

When our daughter Bev came to work for us, that meant I could be home and do more cooking. Chuck would still call me from the office each afternoon and ask what we were going to do for dinner. When I would say I was cooking, his voice would fall, and he would sound disappointed. I never understood why. He used to like my cooking! This went on for a whole year. When I asked him if he liked my cooking, he would say yes, but there was something in his voice I just couldn't figure out.

One Sunday evening I was too tired to go to church, so Chuck went alone. We had gone out for dinner on Friday night, and I had not used the chicken I had thawed. I planned to make him biscuits and gravy, fried chicken. and salad, and thought he would really be pleased. When he came home he came up behind me as I was rolling out the biscuits, put his arms around me, and asked why I was working so hard. *That proves it!* I thought. *He doesn't like my cooking. Forget the gravy!*

At dinner he didn't eat any of my biscuits. Now I knew for sure he didn't like my cooking. I wanted to talk about it right then, but because of all that we had been learning about giving Chuck time to get in touch with his feelings, I decided not to. When we went to bed later I asked the Lord, "Should I talk to Chuck about this?" I heard in my head, *Leave it alone.* I said, "Chuck!"(I was really obedient, wasn't I?). I asked him if he had eaten anything on the way home, and he said no. I pointed out to him that he had not eaten my biscuits at dinner. He said he hadn't noticed any biscuits. I told him I was making them when he hugged me in the kitchen. He had seen me put them in the oven! I again raised the question of his not liking my cooking. He insisted he did, and asked why was I making such a big deal out of this, and said there must be something more going on to make me so angry.

There was! I was reading a book about a man who

who had a worldwide ministry, but was neglecting his family in favor of the ministry. Even though his wife was sick in bed with a nervous breakdown, this man left his family to go and wait in Hawaii for more money to come in so he could get on with his ministry. Then he would write home and tell about all the people who were coming out to hear him speak. I thought, *If Chuck wasn't controlled by the Lord, he would be just like that man.* In fact, in the past Chuck *had* put "ministry" above how I felt. He had changed, but I was identifying so strongly with the wife's situation I forgot about him changing. I was getting more and more angry at Chuck while I was reading the book. That's what was in my heart. We had a "discussion" that night that was really hard. It had become a crisis.

Most of the time a crisis makes the nonexpressive person start thinking. So the next day Chuck called and said, "I know why I don't always want to come home for dinner. The phone is ringing, and you're up and down doing dinner things, and we just don't get to talk like we do when we go out." I said, "Oh, I'll go out to dinner with you anytime!" When you know how the other person really feels, you can handle it. It is *not* knowing that is so hard. We read in Proverbs that "by presumption comes much strife." Both of us have to resist reading a wrong meaning into what the other person says and does.

"Reading into" is called "subjective" thinking. When the subjective person reads into what the other person is saying, he usually assumes the worst. An example of this was the time I was preparing a cheese snack. I like it melted in the microwave. I cut a piece of cheese and was putting it in the microwave when Barb said to me, "Boy that's a big piece of cheese." Since I had been wrestling with an extra twenty pounds for a long time, what I heard was, "Listen,

Chubby, you don't need all that cheese." She swears all she meant was that it would not melt very well in the micro-wave—it would burn the edges before it all melted.

It took a year of Chuck thinking over why I kept asking him about my cooking—and then finally a crisis —before we could talk about this issue and come to an understanding as to why he didn't want to come home for dinner. This is just one more proof to me that nonex-pressive people need time to get in touch with their feelings. Then after they *do* know how they feel, it's im-portant for them to make a date with you to talk about the problem. They seem to think if they don't talk about it, it will just go away. As we've mentioned, when a person stuffs their feelings, the feelings are not dead. It's like putting garbage in a closed container in a warm place. Sooner or later, after it ferments, it explodes. And often the explosion comes when you least expect it, when it doesn't even necessarily fit the occasion.

Once I just tapped on the car window to get Chuck's attention, and he was instantly angry because of all the things he had been stuffing. I told him I didn't feel safe with him, because I never knew when the next explosion would come. I've mentioned that Chuck has a quiet way of "exploding," but I can easily read his body language and his silence.

Everyone needs to feel safe. I knew Chuck was rating me on a performance basis, but I wasn't sure what performance was causing the anger. He did not have unconditional love for me at that time. As long as I performed correctly, I got his approval. When I did something that bothered him, he held back his ap-proval.

One time Chuck was on the phone giving direc-tions to someone. I got his attention and added some details. He got furious. It was one of those times when his anger did not match the situation. Later he came upstairs and apologized, but I felt like staying hurt. He kept his hand on my shoulder (he had never done that before) and insisted we talk about it.

Once again I sound like a real beast, but the phone thing was just a matter of my being more one-dimensional. It's hard for me to do two things at once—like talk on the phone and to Barb at the same time. I hate the phone anyway; I don't know why I even answer it. Furthermore, Barb knows all the details of our life, and the calls are usually for her. Besides, she's the social director. I can't tell you how many times I have gotten in trouble by making unilateral decisions about when and where we would be available for dinner with someone or counseling or some other social activity. Finally I got it through my head that we had to decide together whether the timing was right. Since she had a better feel for that sort of thing anyway, it was easier for us when we talked about it. I had been known to schedule a night out immediately after a very exhausting trip. It looked fine three months prior to the date, but of course as we dragged ourselves off our death bed to keep the commitment, I could see the foolishness of my decision.

Again, personality differences play a part in how we communicate. Some people are passive and some are aggressive, but it's best to be *assertive*, in the right sense. Our culture has changed the meaning of being assertive. Today we think it means aggressively standing up for our rights. But a better meaning is, You tell me how you feel about a situation, and I'll tell you how I feel. It's done with pure motives: We want the best for each other.

I saw a cartoon once in which an announcer on TV said, "Tonight's telethon to benefit the National Inferiority Complex Foundation has been canceled. Our master of ceremonies and the entire staff just went home saying they didn't think they were good enough to do the show." This reminded me of many passive, nonassertive people. They usually have low self-esteem and will not risk saying anything in a situation they don't like until they reach the boiling point. Then they can't help but skip the assertive step; they become aggressive and explode.

The passive person thinks this way: "I have no power, I'm not worth much anyway, I really don't have a right to tell this person what to do, it won't do any good anyway, it's better to just leave it alone, no one will listen to me anyway." The problem with this approach is that the person stuffs his or her feelings, and later on these will come out in an aggressive manner.

On the other hand, the aggressive person says this, in effect: "It's all your fault. You are responsible for my feelings. You made me do that. Since *you're* wrong, *you* should change." The aggressive person seems to care little about the other's feelings. So when his or her anger flares, everyone is in trouble.

Conflict is neither good nor bad, it just is. It's okay to be angry, but the problem comes in how we handle our anger. Do you force someone like Chuck to talk when you realize he can't really tell you how he feels, and pressuring him will only make him feel attacked? On the other hand, do you withdraw in anger when a person like me attacks and gives no hope that the problem will ever be solved?

We don't like to make too many general statements, but it seems that usually it's the man who gets silent and withdraws in a conflict. Unfortunately that has often been the case with me. I'm trying my best to be a better communicator when we need to talk, but it's hard. I've read that silence shows little regard for relationships. It's insulting and demeaning, and leaves the other partner helpless and hopeless. I value Barb as the greatest person in my life besides Jesus Christ, so my silence does not mean I don't value the relationship—I do. I just need more time to get in touch with my feelings.

Even though many men withdraw, it is really more of a temperament difference than a man-woman difference. Sometimes it is the woman who withdraws, but whoever withdraws must stop and see the big picture of how devastating it is for the other person.

Even door slamming in anger has been studied, and this does seem to be a man-woman difference. Research shows that if a woman slams a door in anger, she's usually gone INSIDE—to her bedroom or a bathroom. This means she can't talk about the situation right now, but will get to it later. A man usually slams a door as he goes OUTSIDE. He just wants to get out of there.

Body language is undeniably an important part of communication. When we arrive somewhere together in the car, Chuck often lets me out before parking. When he did this during our hard times, he would sometimes start moving the car forward before I had gotten completely out and closed the car door. I thought, *I'll be killed if he isn't careful.* Through this action Chuck was communicating to me that he wasn't pleased with me.

Studies have shown that 55 percent of communication is through body language; 35 percent through tone of voice; 2 percent is intuitive, and only 8 percent is through words. If body, vocal tone, and words don't match, we have not communicated properly and have given confusing or even dishonest signals.

We might notice our spouse being unusually quiet, and we ask, "Is something wrong?" While looking out the car window in the other direction, our spouse responds, "NO, EVERYTHING IS FINE!" Because body language and tone of voice don't match the words, we know everything isn't fine.

I really think it's harder to be a nonexpressive. I've accused Chuck of "controlling" me, and he is mystified as to how he is doing it. In psychological circles it's called being a "passive aggressive." In our relationship it works like this: When Chuck is ready to go or ready to get out of a situation—especially in a group—he drums his fingers on something, or stretches his arms and legs and moves around in his chair, or stands up, or eventually all three. His body may be there, but he is no where around—especially in a group. I've been asked so many times, "What is wrong with Chuck? Isn't he feeling well?" "No, he's fine. He's just been working hard" (which is true). But basically he's just uncomfortable in that situation. I've asked him to be more "sparkly" when we're out, but it's just not that easy for him, so he gets quiet. Although, once again, if his goals for the time he is spending with someone include teaching or counseling, I can hardly get a word in edgewise.

Barb said she thought it was probably harder to be a nonexpressive, and I can tell you from personal experience it's awful. I hate it when I get silent or withdrawn, and I suffer for it. If I don't get my feelings out verbally, they come out physically. My hands break out when I am under a great deal of stress at home or work. I also get severe headaches, backaches, and neckaches when I'm keeping my emotions in. I guess that's the source of the phrase "You're a pain in the neck! " People can literally be a pain if we don't deal honestly with our feelings toward them. Some of the reading I've done suggests that most people in mental institutions are there because of not adequately facing up to difficult situations in their lives. Many people with real physical ailments are in hospitals because of anger, bitterness, resentment, and other feelings they have suppressed and stuffed. It's dangerous to be a nonexpressive. That's probably why God usually pairs up people like me with an expressive person like Barb, so we have some help in learning to face up to our feelings.

Learn how your mate is designed. If he or she withdraws in conflict, try to become a better listener. If your mate "attacks" in conflict, ask for a little more time to get in touch with your feelings.

Barb thinks the nonexpressive has the hardest job, but I really feel the expressive does—because the nonexpressive is so fragile and can be hurt so easily. So let's put the responsibility for getting the ball rolling on the expressive. Be a better listener, and give your partner time to get in touch with his or her feelings.

And don't forget the banana principle. It really works!

10

A Handle on Anger

(CHUCK:) One of the most common emotions we humans feel is anger. We see it on our freeways, in our churches, in our neighborhoods, at work, and in our marriages. Anger is the core emotion in a divorce. Anger is everywhere—and can be destructive to everyone.

(BARB:) Since anger is so much a part of our discussion, let's see what the Bible says about it.

Let all bitterness and wrath and anger and clamor and slander be put away from you, along with all malice.
(Ephesians 4:31)

I see in this verse a progression of anger, especially as it relates to conflicts in our marriage relationships. It describes what happens when we don't handle our hurts and our anger properly. Let's take a look at the major words in the verse.

Notice the significant progression as we examine these words in the same order Paul lists them:

"Bitterness"—This is a cutting, pricking sharpness. As a human emotion it's the feeling of hatred, resentment, and cynicism, as in Hebrews 12:15. It's on the INSIDE of us, although others can usually detect it even when we think we're hiding it.

"Wrath"—Now the bitterness shows itself clearly on the OUTSIDE. "Wrath" is agitation with a passion. *Vine's Expository Dictionary of Greek Words* depicts it as hot, fierce, and outbursting.

"Anger"—If the conflict is unsettled, it goes back on the INSIDE. "Anger" connotes an inward, impulsive feeling, frequently with a view to taking revenge. The other person may think the conflict was solved with the blowup, but in reality it wasn't.

"Clamor"—Suddenly, when everything seems to be going well in the relationship, something sets one person off again, and the conflict is back on the OUTSIDE. The anger has progressed to clamor—that is, "an outcry," or as *Vine's* describes it, "a tumult of controversy." This is when we say, "But we talked about this. Why are you bringing it up again? We just keep going over and over the same thing." Actually the problem had really never been solved in the first place.

"Slander"—This means "evil speaking." *Vine's* calls it "railing." In Greek it has the root words *blapto*, meaning "to injure," and *pheme*, which means "speech." This is where we just don't care what we say about the other person—if it hurts…who cares?

"Malice"—This means wickedness, "an active ill-will." *Vine's* says it is "a badness in quality, vicious in character." It's the actual desire to harm another person. It means "spite," and "evil intent." The angry person, being deeply hurt, plans how to get back at the other person. And so…there's a divorce.

Can you see where it all starts? By wanting our own way. By wanting to be served rather than serving each other. By thinking more highly of ourselves than we ought to think. By not being obedient. And what is it we are not obeying? The very next verse in Ephesians 4 gives us this command:

And be kind to one another, tender-hearted, forgiving each other just as God in Christ also has forgiven you.

In other words, we are to serve one another. We have to deny ourselves with humility and obedience. I wish there was another way, because this one is so hard.

As I've thought about what it means to quench and grieve the Holy Spirit, I've seen that quenching the Spirit results from not doing what God tells you to do. No one else may know that you are being urged by Him to do something, such as asking someone's forgiveness, but *you* know it. Yet you refuse to do what you know God asks you to do. To others you seem to be perfectly in control and "holy," but on the inside you are being passively disobedient.

Grieving the Holy Spirit, on the other hand, comes from doing what the Lord tells you *not* to do. It is having a blowup when the Lord says, "Be quiet." It is screaming and stomping around when you know it's not right. It is initiating the divorce, or moving in with someone else because your husband is so awful. Quenching the Holy Spirit is passive, and grieving the Holy Spirit is aggressive. Quenching is on the inside with bitterness or impulsive anger. Grieving is on the outside with wrath, clamor, slander and malice.

Obedience, on the other hand, is kindness, tender-heartedness, and forgiveness.

As Barb indicated, anger is one of the chief emotions evident when you talk to people who are contemplating divorce.

There's so much anger in the world. Just drive a few miles down the freeway and you'll see plenty evidence of that.

Anger has four basic causes, according to the book *Facing Anger* by Norman Rohrer and Philip Sutherland. The first is the desire to feel powerful. If our behavior is determined by other people, we feel weak. The person who feels powerful doesn't need anger, but the weak person needs it to restore power. There are power struggles between husbands and wives over such things as spending and saving money, disciplining the kids, decorating the home, where to take vacations, and conflicting careers. There are power struggles between parents and children over such things as cleaning rooms, emptying the garbage, bedtime hours, dating, the type of friends the kids have, and allowances.

Philippians 4:11-13 gives us the key to dealing with power struggles:

Not that I was ever in need, for I have learned how to get along happily whether I have much or little. I know how to live on almost nothing or with everything. I have learned the secret of contentment in every situation, whether it be a full stomach or hunger, plenty or want; for I can do everything God asks me to with the help of Christ who gives me the strength and power.

A contented person is not the one who has everything, but the one who desires nothing.

The second basic cause of anger is feeling self-sufficient. Kids want to put on their own socks, have their own car, choose their own clothes. We all need each other. Self-sufficiency keeps people from seeking help from doctors and counselors, and from asking for financial help. When we can't do it ourselves, we become angry. Here are some biblical principles relating to self-sufficiency:

As God's messenger I give each of you God's warning: Be honest in your estimate of yourselves, measuring your value by how much faith God has given you. Just as there are many parts to our bodies, so it is with Christ's body. We are all parts of it, and it takes every one of us to make it complete, for we each have different work to do. So we belong to each other, and each needs all the others. (Romans 12:3-5)

What are you so puffed up about? What do you have that God hasn't given you? And if all you have is from God, why act as though you are so great, and as though you have accomplished something on your own? (1 Corinthians 4:7)

Overcoming self-sufficiency is especially hard for people in the public eye. Our athlete friends, for instance, are so talented in their sport. The world worships sports and if the athletes aren't careful, they'll begin to think they had something to do with their talent. God is the one who gave them their athletic gifts.

Even Christians who become ministry "superstars" are tempted to read their own press clippings. They start out with a fantastic calling, and change people's lives in mighty ways. Because people are touched, they come up to the superstars and tell them how wonderful they are. Rather than pointing to Christ, they say in effect: "I guess I AM something special," and they begin expecting people to serve them, give them deals, put them at the head table, cater to their needs, and give them stretch limos to ride in. This is one of the greatest traps in ministry—thinking we have accomplished something on our own.

The Bible says this:

Although being a know-it-all makes us feel important, what is really needed to build the church is love. If anyone thinks he knows all the answers, he is just showing his ignorance. But the person who truly loves God is the one who is open to God's knowledge. (1 Corinthians 8:1-3)

We need to protect ourselves from any "us four and no more" type of thinking. So many people get trapped into narrow doctrinal positions, or styles of worship that exclude others if they don't fit the same mold. The church (which is people, not a building) needs massive doses of love to carry out its mission in this world—to be "Christ" to the hurting people in the street. I love the song "And They'll Know We Are Christians by Our Love." How powerful! If we aren't loving, then where's proof that the Spirit of Christ is really in us?

Self-sufficient people have a hard time loving and being loved. They are usually loners and hard to work with. One of the greatest gifts we can give each other is to admit when we are wrong and ask forgiveness. Fathers especially need to learn how to ask for forgiveness from their wives and kids. It's usually we men who fail the most in trying to be self-sufficient. We have the hardest time admitting our mistakes.

The next basic cause of anger is the desire to feel important. In everything we want to be first in line, chairman, president, captain and winner. When we lose, we get angry and depressed. Depression, remember, is often anger turned inward toward ourselves. Our society frowns on murder, so when we get mad at our boss or neighbor or child or mate, and then keep our anger within—this makes us blue. Here are more Scriptures that can help us when we need to feel important:

"Anyone wanting to be a leader among you must be your servant. And if you want to be right at the top, you must serve like a slave. Your attitude must be like my own, for I, the Messiah, did not come to be served, but to serve, and to give my life as a ransom for many." (Matthew 20:26-28)

As Barb explained earlier, our highest calling as a Christian is to serve, for in this way we become a true example of Christ to the world.

"The more lowly your service to others, the greater you are. To be the greatest, be a servant. But those who think themselves great

*shall be disappointed and humbled; and those who humble them-
selves shall be exalted."* (Matthew 23:11-12)

*For, dear brothers, you have been given freedom: not freedom to
do wrong, but freedom to love and serve each other. For the whole
Law can be summed up in this one command: Love others as you
love yourself. But if instead of showing love among yourselves
you are always critical and catty, watch out. Beware of ruining
each other.* (Galatians 5:13-15)

This is one of the areas where my early church training
failed me. I thought God was a God of rules and restric-
tions. I felt Christianity was a life of bondage, not freedom.
Then I learned that God's law gives us freedom—the freedom to love. And if I love you, I surely am not going to
steal from you, commit adultery with your wife, lie to you,
or cheat you in some way. Love releases me from all that.
Now I can love and serve you with the freedom Christ
gives me. He releases my spirit to love, to put you first, to
meet your needs, to ask your forgiveness when I don't want
to, to do loving things for my wife even when I don't feel
like it. God's love is inexhaustible, and we've only sampled
a very small part of it here on this earth. How exciting to
look forward to the day when we'll experience the fullness
of His love. I can hardly wait!

*You younger men, follow the leadership of those who are older.
And all of you serve each other with humble spirits, for God gives
special blessings to those who are humble, but sets himself
against those who are proud. If you will humble yourselves under
the mighty hand of God, in his good time he will lift you up.* (1
Peter 5:5-6)

It's not wrong to have a need to feel important. We all
need approval, and to be allowed to have feelings. Actually,
until we have acknowledged a person's feelings, we have
not really acknowledged the person, and that's true in how

we view ourselves as well. What we have to work on is giving our feelings to God when people fail us and make us feel unimportant.

The fourth thing that makes us angry is the desire to be perfect. We want to be a straight-A student and get angry when the teacher gives us a B. The concert pianist gets angry when she hits a wrong note. The baseball player gets angry when he strikes out. The football player feels it when he misses a block.

Sometimes we have a need to be perfect so we'll feel accepted. A perfectionist's standards are way too high. If they do ninety-nine things right and one wrong—they are angry. It carries over into their attitude toward others as well. The kids don't mow the lawn right, or they leave spots when they wash the car, and the perfectionist parent gets angry.

A perfectionist views the world as right or wrong, black or white, cold or hot, up or down. When we have this view, we defend our positions with anger when we can't admit our failures, because we have the need to be perfect.

But so much of life has no perfect or "right" answers —such as our differing tastes in food, music, art, cars, home decorating, hair styles and clothes. Even the types of worship we prefer in church are examples of DIFFERENT approaches, not wrong approaches. Here's some Scripture to help us in this:

If you are angry, don't sin by nursing your grudge. Don't let the sun go down with you still angry—get over it quickly; for when you are angry you give a mighty foothold to the devil. (Ephesians 4:26-27)

We have to be careful not to misread this, because we nonexpressives are in big trouble if we take this literally to mean we sin if we haven't solved our problem before the sun goes down. Sometimes we need a day or two to even figure out why we're angry and what the problem really is. I think what this verse means is to AGREE to solve the problem. Make a date to talk about it. Give the expressive person hope that you will think about it and talk about it when you get in touch with your feelings.

When you nonexpressives go to bed still unable to put words to your feelings, just reach out and touch your expressive partner, and say, "I'm still committed, and we will resolve this problem, but I need some time."

Here's a Scripture that nails me to the wall, one of those that's especially good for framing and hanging by the bathroom mirror:

Stop being mean, bad-tempered and angry. Quarreling, harsh words, and dislike of others should have no place in your lives. Instead, be kind to each other, tenderhearted, forgiving one another, just as God has forgiven you because you belong to Christ. (Ephesians 4:31)

If we all would appropriate this each time we have conflict in a marriage, there would be no divorces.

Let's take another look at 1 Peter 3:7 (in the *New American Standard Bible* here), which tells us how a husband should view his wife:

You husbands likewise, live with your wives in an understanding way, as with a weaker vessel, since she is a woman; and grant her honor as a fellow heir of the grace of life, so that your prayers may not be hindered.

In other words, we are to figure out what makes her like she is. To live in understanding, we have to pay attention, do some research as to what she needs, find out what makes her tick.

One of the hardest things to understand about a woman is the emotional messages she sends. I miss more of these than I catch, unfortunately. Barb and I have had conflicts in which she will say something like, "Just get out of here!" Now to my computer brain, that means go to my shop, go to work, go to the hardware store. But what she really means is, "Stay here, take me in your arms, fight through my tears and raised voice, and show me how valuable I am to you." When I walk away I'm telling her I don't value the relationship very much at that particular moment. The result is that emotionally she doesn't feel very important. But by my staying—by not being put off by the tone of her voice or the literal meaning of her words or the surface message in her body language—I am telling her that she *is* important and that I intend to stay right there until the conflict is resolved.

Let me tell you right now, this is almost impossible for me to do. I'm trying to improve in this area for Barb, and I'll keep working at it, but it will take God's strength to do it.

We're studying meekness and anger in the coaches' Bible study I teach on Thursdays, and we had a great discussion last time as I was giving the guys both barrels on how they should live in meekness (strength under control) and handle their anger, etc. I had been having a fairly even time in my life, so I could "preach" with great fervor about what my friends should do. Then things blew up that night between Barb and me, and we both were put through the wringer.

The next morning I was to have breakfast with the University of Washington football team, for whom Barb and I serve as chaplains. It's just one of those things you have to do when you're on the mission field—eat steak with the troops. (We've also been with the Huskies to four postseason bowls so far, and so in each of those years had our mission field relocated for two midwinter weeks in Hawaii, Florida, Southern California, and Texas. It's a tough job, but someone has to do it.)

Anyway, that morning I jumped in my very dependable car and took off. The gas gauge was a little low, but I had seen it register lower when I still had plenty left. Then some guy in front of me stopped right in the middle of the street on a downhill slope. My motor stopped and wouldn't start because I was headed downhill and there was no gas suction. I walked home to get the spare can of gas I have in the garage and asked Barb to run me down to where the car was, and I would quickly be on my way. The gas cans were empty, so I had to go to our friendly Texaco just up the street—which was closed. I then had to go to a friendly Chevron a mile or so away. I filled the cans and we drove to where my ailing car was sitting with the flasher lights warning folks to just go around. It was right in the middle of an intersection so it wasn't a matter of just letting it sit. I had been able to coast it partially up on the curb, but it was sitting at quite an angle with the gas cap down. I remembered to bring along a funnel, but it was the wrong type of funnel to use when the car was sitting at an angle. Over Barb's objections, I drove to a hardware store to get the right kind of funnel. She wanted me to go to a gas station and borrow one. How could I do that when I didn't plan to buy anything? I bought the funnel, we put in the gas, and it still wouldn't start because the battery was run down.

I took Barb home, called a tow truck, and walked back to the car to wait. Finally the tow truck came, but the service station where we took it was really busy and they couldn't get to it for a few hours. We had to get to the stadium for the pregame ceremonies, so I called Barb to pick me up. She was not home. She had gone to get gas in our other car because it was low, too. I started to walk again, only this time it was several miles back home. After walking awhile I passed another phone booth so I called again. This time Barb was in the shower—so I walked some more. In the meantime a guest had shown up forty-five minutes early at home. Our dog Muffit had urped a couple of times on the rug, Barb was trying to get ready for the game, plus having to come get me. We finally lived through the day, and picked up the car $66 poorer because some guy stopped when he didn't have to—and after the game I went to bed early with a headache.

You know why all this happened, don't you? I gave you a hint earlier. The Lord was just checking me out to see if I could handle anger and difficulties with as much grace and meekness as I was asking the coaches in the Bible study to do. I'm proud to report that I was ninety-two percent successful. Barb and I felt tight a couple of times, but I was really grateful that the car had not stopped on the floating bridge, that Barb was home to help, that it wasn't raining, that it wasn't midnight, that I hadn't been in a wreck. I had so much to be thankful for despite the hassle and frustration of things not going well. Barb's schedule had been worse than mine that week, but she held up wonderfully.

This is a dumb little story to tell you, but my purpose is to warn you that often the Lord will check us out in the areas in which we are comfortable, just to see if we can walk our talk.

There's a wonderful book on anger by Robert Eliot and Dennis Breo with the title *Is It Worth Dying For?* The book's last lines read:

1. Don't sweat the small stuff.
2. It's all small stuff.

I love that. It really puts everything in perspective, doesn't it?

11

It's Just a Little Brain Damage

(CHUCK:) Some of the differences between men and women are the results of temperament, culture and heredity. Some, however, are God-designed. Our different brain wiring is one of them.

Among those who have studied this inborn mental difference is Dr. Donald Joy, who talked about it in a *Focus on the Family* radio interview. I don't pretend to have all the details, but the big picture is this: Evidently the brain in a male fetus is bathed with a hormone early in its development that destroys many of the interconnecting fibers between the two halves of the brain. A female fetus does not experience this, so she is born with all these interconnecting fibers intact.

One of the results of this is to make a man more one-dimensional. That doesn't mean he can't use both sides of his brain. It simply means he normally is using only one side at a time. He moves back and forth, depending on what he is working on—figuring math problems or learning a language or examining details with the left side of his brain, and painting a picture, listening to music, or writing with his right side.

One example of this would be Monday Night Football. Let's say I'm watching the Seattle Seahawks maul the Chicago Bears (a little fantasy never hurt anyone)—okay, I am watching Seattle squeak by the Colts. It is an important game and I am really into it. All of a sudden I am vaguely aware of a disturbance in the room. My mind snaps away from the game to discover Barb is trying to communicate with me. I always advise wives not to try to talk with their husbands until halftime, but here is Barb trying to get my attention to tell me that the roof blew off, the cat had nineteen kittens, a child is trapped in a tree, or some other insignificant household detail.

She finally gets loud enough to break through my concentration on the game. You see, I don't know I am married, or have three kids, or a cat, or a roof, or live in the United States. All I know is that if Curt Warner doesn't make third and long, the team and I are in big trouble! Wives, believe me, your husband is completely innocent. Yet there have been wives who have resorted to cutting remarks like "You never hear anything I say" or "You don't love me anymore" or "Can we talk?" He loves her, and if that ever changes he will let her know. Right now he's watching a football game and cannot communicate and watch at the same time. And you wives fail us terribly when just as you get our attention you huff out the door saying, "Well, if you didn't hear me, you can just forget dinner!" He's innocent. He didn't even know you existed.

Or there are those times when I am reading the paper at breakfast. I don't even know Barb is out of bed yet, but all of a sudden I glance up and she's sitting at the table saying something like "Isn't that right?" or "What do you think about that?" Again, I didn't even know I had a wife. I was into my paper.

Here's the way to solve this problem, wives, and it's worth the price of the book itself. When you want his attention for something, just take his head in your hands and look into his eyes. They will be glazed over a bit, but don't panic. Then say something like, "Testing, testing—Barb to Chuck, Barb to Chuck." Then the eyes will unglaze, he will see that you exist, and you can tell him anything you want. Just make sure you have his attention before you speak.

By way of contrast, when Barb and I go to a Mariners baseball game she takes along her cross-stitch. For nine innings she not only watches the game and does her cross-stitch, but also talks to several of the player's wives (and knows which of them are angry, which are pregnant, and which are lonely); and at any given moment she can tell you both the score of the game and the exact location of Rick the peanut guy. Meanwhile, all I know is that if Harold Reynolds doesn't get on base, we stand to lose the game. This is because I am just working on one side of my brain at a time, and Barb is working on both sides of hers at once. This makes her more aware and sensitive to what is going on. Some husbands are threatened with this "women's intuition." I have learned to thank God for it. Barb helps me be more sensitive.

This difference between men and women also prevents husbands from finding things easily. Women, have you ever asked your husband to get the little widget from your dressing table? He goes to look for it, but comes back empty-handed. "It just isn't there," he reports. So you drop your kumquats or the report you're working on for the next day, and lo and behold, the widget is right where you thought it was. Don't worry about it; your husband just has a little brain damage.

Barb and I take quite a few vitamin pills at our age. (If I ever bump off, be sure to check the pill box. I take anything she gives me—chalk, buttons, pins—I never look, I just swallow. Barb could easily slip in some arsenic or something. I'm not saying she would, but it's something you might check if I mysteriously disappear.) When I report to Barb that the aluminum pills are low, I'll add, "But don't get up; I'll find the new bottle." I go to the cupboard and, as I suspected, they are not there. Barb then gets up, MOVES THINGS AROUND in the cupboard, and soon finds what I was looking for. I never thought about moving anything. Somehow I thought it should always be in the front row.

It's the same situation when Barb wants me to get something out of the refrigerator. I search, but come back empty-handed; Barb goes over and—right behind the moldy macaroni and cheese—there it is, plain as day. Again, I didn't even THINK about moving anything around. Blame it on brain damage.

The worst thing, though, is when the wife asks the husband to find something, and he reports a no-find, and then she goes to look and can't find it either. Instead of being on the dressing table, it's on the bedside table. Rather than apologizing, most wives in this situation will degrade the husband for not looking around a little more. Or, worse than that, they will tee-hee and giggle and make a big joke about thinking it was somewhere it wasn't. That's enough to drive you nutty. It's World War III when YOU don't find something, but when SHE can't find it either, it's the comedy hour. Sounds like a double standard to me.

Or there are those times when she swears she told you something and you are equally as sure that those words never came out of her mouth in your presence. Perhaps she talked about it with her mom, her girlfriend, the butcher, the neighbor—but she has never once brought up the subject within your hearing range. Barb sometimes just THINKS about something and later is sure she mentioned it to me. My feeling is that I'm SURE I would have remembered something THAT important if she had told me.

Wives do not give proper introductions and transitions in their conversations, either. We'll be driving along in the car talking about Aunt Suzie's haircut and all of a sudden Barb will be giving some details that have nothing to do with the subject at hand. I'll listen to a little bit of it, and ask what that has to do with Aunt Suzie's haircut, and Barb is already talking about Uncle Ted's violin, but has failed to let me know. Or she will be talking about how wonderful Larry is so I'm going along with her in my mind agreeing that Larry Cyphers is a great person, when all of a sudden she will mention his home in Twisp. Larry doesn't live in Twisp, so I challenge her. I find out that she is talking about Larry Parker. He's also a great guy but I have to then go back over the whole conversation and bring my brain up to date with the new name. She thinks it should be obvious to me who she is talking about.

Once we were driving on our way to speak at a retreat and chatting about things back home, and Barb said something like, "You'll really enjoy meeting her." I wondered how "her" got into the conversation. Does she come to our class at church? Is she a new neighbor, or someone new in Barb's Bible study group? As it turned out, the "her" was a Kathy who would be at the retreat. For me to know that right from the start, all Barb would have had to say was, "When we get to the retreat you will enjoy meeting Kathy." But see what a wilderness it leads me into when she forgets the first six words and the name?

I know you can't relate to all this, and I am the only man in the world who can't follow his wife's train of thought at all times. But I share this with you so you can pray for me. I've got a little brain damage.

12

Smoke Comes Out My Ears

(CHUCK:) Now we want to talk about a very misunderstood biblical concept—one that for many people raises the hackles (whatever hackles are) on the back of the neck, elevates the blood pressure, and makes smoke come out the ears.

The word for it is *submission*. It's a concept that has often been abused over the years, especially by men.

Ephesians 5 is one of the basic Scriptures that shed light on this concept. Most men will start reading at verse 22, where it says, "You wives must submit to your husband's leadership in the same way you submit to the Lord." To a man that sounds great. This means I make all the final decisions in the family and determine all the vacation sites and who takes out the garbage and what time my wife will have dinner ready, etc.

We have a problem, however, when we back up one verse and read, "Honor Christ by submitting to EACH

OTHER." That makes the situation less clear-cut than I thought it was. This verse presents a TEAM relationship, rather than one member lording it over the other.

We mentioned earlier that men often misunderstand the concept of leadership, the biblical meaning of which is "servanthood." So, rather than make our family conform to our every whim, it appears that it is WE who should be conforming to the needs of our family.

(BARB:) I've thought so much about how to present this. It will not be easy for you to read—nor will it be easy to put into practice. However, what I am going to show you is the key to having a great marriage even if you feel you and your mate are incompatible. We are all so different, and often we can't agree on the things we want. Even this last week, I found myself angry with Chuck because his values were not my values. I had to deny myself to serve him, but I wanted him to deny himself also.

The most important consideration is your heart attitude. Do we want to serve ourselves or serve the Lord? Are we committed to ourselves or to Jesus Christ? Are we sold out to doing things our own way, or are we sold out to doing what God wants us to do?

I often think of the Scripture that tells us to cast all our anxiety on Him because He cares for us. Just before that, He has told us to humble ourselves before Him so He can exalt us. He knows that often we'd rather not do things His way. But He tells us, "Don't worry, I care for you, I won't tell you to do anything that won't turn out for your good." Even the things we consider bad will ultimately be for our good. Someone has said that the Lord may hurt us, but He will never harm us. Chuck and I have had to hurt for a while in order to find peace with each other. But in the long run, only good has come from the hurt, never harm.

We are told over and over again in the Bible to follow Christ's example. Jesus Himself says:

"You call Me Teacher and Lord; and you are right; for so I am. If I then, the Lord and the Teacher, washed your feet, you also ought to wash one another's feet. For I gave you an example that you also should do as I did to you. Truly, truly, I say to you, a slave is not greater than his master; neither one who is sent greater than the one who sent him. If you know these things, you are blessed if you do them."
(John 13:13-17)

So, you see, we are to follow His example, and when we do that we will be blessed. He wasn't teaching us to wash feet. He was teaching us how to serve. He came to love unconditionally, which means He loves us no matter what we've done in the past, or what we do in the future. The question we have to ask ourselves is, Do I have the same attitude—to love and to serve?

Chuck and I have been asked, "What is the primary message you feel the Lord has given you, the concept that stands out most in your minds?" At first I talked about serving one another, and of course that is key. But then I thought—if we had never been obedient to what we read in Scripture and what we knew the Lord wanted us to do, we would know nothing about serving.

One of the reasons we don't want to obey is that we are sure the Lord wants to put us in a prison of some kind. We don't realize that He sets parameters around us to set us free. We think the Ten Commandments were given to bind us up. But we have missed the point completely. They were given to set us free—both in our relationship with the Lord and with one another. The Old Testament law talks about loving the Lord our God with all our mind, with all our soul,

and with all our strength, and our neighbor as ourselves. Is it worth it? Look at the promised results:

*But the one who looks intently at the perfect law, the law of
liberty, and abides by it, not having become a forgetful
hearer but an effectual doer, this man shall be blessed in
what he does.* (James 1:25)

So we must look into the law intently and know
what the Bible says. We must remember what it says,
and do it. Then God will bless us in what we do.

In Jesus' words in John 12:26 we again see a blessing in the form of honor:

*"If anyone serves Me, let him follow Me...if anyone serves
Me, the Father will honor him."*

The reason this is so hard is it's talking about a lifetime commitment to the Lord rather than to ourselves.
Jesus made this very clear:

*"If anyone wishes to come after Me, let him deny himself,
and take up his cross, and follow Me."* (Mark 8:34)

The Greek verbs translated "deny" and "take up
his cross" in this verse are in a tense that indicates an
action we decide to do at one point in time, and then
make it a continuing goal for the rest of our life.
"Follow me" is in the present tense, which means to
keep on following. We are to keep on following because we've made it a lifetime goal.

All these principles relate to what the roles of a
husband and wife should be in a marriage. We make it
a lifetime goal to submit to each other.

And be subject to one another in the fear of Christ. (Ephesians 5:21)

This is mutual submission—not just the woman

submitting to the man, but the man submitting to the woman also. The reason? Because you've made a lifetime goal to follow Christ. The word "fear" means a wholesome dread of ever displeasing the Lord. Because you know He is your Creator, and that He knows the beginning from the end, and that He rules over all, you don't want to do anything that would displease Him. The controlling motive of your life is to do what He says. Therefore you submit to each other because you love the Lord.

Picture a triangle with God at the top, a husband at one of the lower corners, and a wife at the other. When you are not submitting to each other, the two of you at the bottom of the triangle draw farther apart. The further you get from each other, the further you are from the Lord.

Our grandchild Kjersten watches *Sesame Street* and is in love with Big Bird, so we bought an animated Big Bird for her birthday. It has an audio tape that tells a story as its eyes blink and its beak moves. After she opened the package, she just sat on the rug in awe of that bird. She would reach out and gently touch Big Bird. Then she would kiss its beak. Then she gently lifted Big Bird into her arms and carried him all over the house while he was telling her a story. We thought—wouldn't it be wonderful if people cared that much about God and what He says? Wouldn't it be wonderful if we loved Him so much that we would submit to one another because He told us to?

The Greek word for "submit" is a military term. It means to rank under. It would be like the relationship between a general and a colonel. An even better example would be a king presiding over a council of other kings. One is not inferior to another; they just have different roles.

The following verses show us how we are to

submit. When we are in the roles the Lord gave us, our partner feels loved, because these roles fulfill each other's needs. The roles of men and women are different, because we have different needs.

The man is to be the provider. God said to Adam:

"Because you have listened to the voice of your wife, and have eaten from the tree about which I commanded you, saying, 'You shall not eat from it'; Cursed is the ground because of you; in toil you shall eat of it all the days of your life. Both thorns and thistles it shall grow for you; and you shall eat the plants of the field; by the sweat of your face you shall eat bread, till you return to the ground, because from it you were taken; for you are dust and to dust you shall return." (Genesis 3:17-19)

On the other hand, a woman is to be a worker at home. Paul in Titus 2:5 commands young women *"to be sensible, pure, workers at home."*

With all the talk of equality between the sexes, our thinking has gotten quite distorted. Young people do not think a woman can be fulfilled being home with the children. In order to be fulfilled our culture says a woman must have a job outside the home. Even young men feel they need help providing for the family. The problem is when young mothers go to work, their husbands and children are left wanting. Scripture does not say a woman cannot work outside the home. In fact, the woman in Proverbs 31 was quite a business woman. But her home was in order and well cared for.

The Greek word translated in Titus as "worker" can also be translated "keeper" or "guardian" of the home. A woman's primary responsibility is the home. Even when we work in the marketplace, we still feel the need for everything to be in order at home. This is a God-given feeling and responsibility.

On the other hand, when a man has been laid off,

or retired too soon, or has nothing to do, his sense of worth suffers. This is because providing for his family is HIS God given feeling and responsibility.

The man is to be the protector.

For the husband is the head of the wife, as Christ also is the head of the church, He Himself being the Savior of the body. (Ephesians 5:23)

Christ is the example of the perfect protector. He guides us even when we walk in darkness. I love it when Chuck guides me across the street with his hand on my back. Or when we're in a large group and he keeps touching me, letting me know he is there and giving me that feeling of protection. He shows his protection in so many ways. He takes care to see that my car is in good shape. He keeps the sidewalks free of snow in the winter. He always checks to see if I've left the iron on before we go to bed. My dad died this last spring, and I know this is one of the things about Dad that Mom misses most. He watched out for her and she knew he cared because of his protection.

From this same Scripture, we see that the man is to be the head of the wife as Christ also is the head of the church. We've already talked about what true headship is when we talked about the servant-leader. Again, Christ is our example. He served rather than lording it over other people. Husbands need to do the same thing.

Most men think they're going to be served when they get married. For that matter, maybe we all want to be served. But remember, "God's ways are not our ways." What happens when we serve is that we will eventually be served in return. Being served, however, should not be our motivation for serving; it's just one of the Lord's pleasant surprises.

Next we see that the woman is to be in submission to the headship of the man:

Wives, be subject to your own husbands, as to the Lord."
(Ephesians 5:22)

Be sure to note that we are to be subject to our *own* husband. We get in lots of trouble listening to someone else's husband.

Here are some examples of true submission by Jesus Christ.

"And He who sent Me is with Me; he has not left Me alone, for I always do the things that are pleasing to Him." (John 8:29)

True submission is doing what pleases your mate. When I know how Chuck feels about something, I can make a decision without consulting him. However, if I don't know his heart, then I wait until we have talked. He does the same thing for me. He was not showing true submission when he was making investments on his own. If I went out and spent money that I knew Chuck didn't want me to spend, that would not be true submission. True submission is looking out for the other. It is serving. Again, Jesus is our example:

"For I have come down from heaven, not to do My own will, but the will of Him who sent Me." (John 6:38)

"I can do nothing on My own initiative. As I hear, I judge; and My judgment is just, because I do not seek My own will, but the will of Him who sent Me." (John 5:30)

If we seek the will of the Father, we can have good judgment too. True submission is not doing your own thing, but doing the will of your husband.

The question often comes up: "If I am in submission will I never again be independent? Can I ever make independent decisions again?" The answer is no.

That's what marriage is all about—two people becoming one, never again making solo decisions. When we get married, we usually are not sure just what our responsibilities are going to be, but we enter into covenant with each other. That means we are responsible to each other, we are to care for one another, and to put the other one before ourselves.

But do I lose all my authority when I am in submission? Jesus' words about the authority He received from His Father are instructive for us:

"And He gave Him authority to execute judgment, because He is the Son of Man." (John 5:27)

Because I am Chuck's wife, I have his authority. But I'm not going to abuse that authority. Hopefully, I am only going to do those things that please him.

Some people worry about being inferior if they are submissive. But was Jesus Christ inferior to God? Hardly! Jesus could tell the religious leaders of His day,

"I and the Father are one." (John 10:30)

When two people marry, they become one flesh. Neither one is above the other. Galatians 3:28 makes this clear:

There is neither Jew nor Greek, there is neither slave nor free man, there is neither male nor female; for you are all one in Christ Jesus.

This verse speaks specifically about the equality of all Christians, whether male or female. The Lord never speaks of one person as superior to another in any human relationship—and that includes marriage.

When a husband is in headship over the wife, and when a wife is in submission to her husband, it is a loving relationship. God is the husband's example of loving rulership. He does not rule with a rod of iron but with a scepter of love. Christ is our example of loving submission, doing only those things that please the Father.

Scripture also teaches that the woman was created to complete her husband:

Then the Lord God said, "It is not good for the man to be alone; I will make him a helper suitable for him." (Genesis 2:18)

This word "helper" has also been misunderstood. It means one who corresponds to him. One who is his completer. I often think of how God gave this gift to man and he's been trying to refuse it ever since.

As we've been discussing, men and women are not the same. We do have different views and opinions, and that is precisely the point. We bring strengths to the relationship that our partners do not have.

If I was the only one writing this book, you probably would not laugh as much, because I do not have the sense of humor Chuck has. Also I don't see as many practical perspectives as Chuck does. But together we are both stronger. Together we present a more balanced picture. The key to this, however, has been our learning to accept each other's differences.

Besides being a completer, the woman is also in the supporting role:

For indeed man was not created for the woman's sake, but woman for the man's sake. (1 Corinthians 11:9)

I know this comes as a shock to many of you women. Scripture says we are to support our husbands. But don't take this wrong. I find great joy in supporting Chuck. When he is content, I am content.

When I push my way with him, and I know he is not happy, then I'm not happy either. It's just not worth it. Our culture is telling women to do their own thing. Scripture tells us just the opposite.

This might seem like a hard message, women, but just stick with me a little longer. I think you'll see the big picture—and like what you see.

The man is to love in an unconditional, initiating way. The woman is to love in a friendly, responding way. Here's what Scripture says about this:

Husbands, love your wives, just as Christ also loved the church and gave Himself up for her. (Ephesians 5:25)

Older women likewise…teaching what is good, that they may encourage the young women to love their husbands, to love their children. (Titus 2:3-4)

Husbands are told to love their wives with an *agape* love.This is a Greek word for unconditional, sacrificial love. This is the kind of love with which Christ loved us when He died for us while we were yet sinners. We did not have to perform for Him to win His love. He initiated it. We love Him because He first loved us. In the same way, when I gain weight, Chuck does not love me less. When I get angry, he doesn't cut off his love for me.

When we were younger, though, Chuck sometimes would walk away from me if my voice got too tight or too high–pitched with emotion. He would say, "You should just hear yourself." He was not giving me unconditional love. I had to "shape up" before we could talk any further. I agree I needed shaping up occasionally; but when I did it, it was out of fear, not respect. I just knew I had to perform to get his approval, because if I didn't he would withdraw his love. Chuck did not know his love was supposed to be unconditional.

When he found out this is what God commands, he changed and no longer responded to me on a performance basis.

Here's how God asks men to love:

So husbands ought also to love their own wives as their own bodies. He who loves his own wife loves himself for no one ever hated his own flesh, but nourishes and cherishes it, just as Christ does the church. (Ephesians 5:28-29)

Our bodies are very important to us, and we make sure they are taken care of. We clothe them, keep them warm, feed them, and treat them in a special way. A wife is supposed to be just as important to her husband as his own body—in fact, so important that he would "give up his life" for her.

Chuck has given up his life for me so many times. Take for instance the tennis court cover he wanted so badly. He isn't angry because I don't want to put a warehouse on our property. He doesn't always agree with me, but he doesn't make my life miserable just because we don't see eye to eye. He has given up something important in his life in order to make me happy. I know I am more important to him than a cover for the tennis court.

Another way he gives up his life is by not setting three alarm clocks to go off fifteen minutes apart in the morning. He likes to get up gradually, and he enjoys knowing that the first two mean he still has a little more time to sleep. Earlier in our marriage I would hear the alarms but just go back to sleep, but later I began staying awake after the first one went off, while Chuck would go back to sleep each time. When I finally told him about the problem, he didn't fuss and fume around. He just started to get up after the first one. It's called adjusting. It's also called serving.

There are ways I show Chuck unconditional love,

too, but he does a better job of it. Actually the kind of love I am to show Chuck is a different kind of love. It's an affectionate love, a responding love. It is seeing something in another person you admire. It is trying to have the same interests. Having things in common attracts you to another person. Because this is not an unconditional love, it is more fragile.

In effect, all Christians are asked to love each other with an *agape* or unconditional love, so wives do not get out from under that obligation, but we are asked also to have more of a responding love to our husbands. Chuck initiates and I respond. Once the good circle of love gets going, it's hard to tell who is doing which kind of love.

A wife is told to love her husband with what in Greek is called *phileo* love. It is friendship love. As I've mentioned, it is seeing in another person something you especially like and enjoy. It's having a fondness for and an attraction for someone. When you have this kind of love you make fun with and for the person. You flirt with him, laugh with him, and look in his eyes, and admire, value, prize, and pay attention to him. What man couldn't love a wife unconditionally who treated him like that?

Both *agape* and *phileo* love involve putting the other person before yourself. Scripture suggests several practical ways we can do this as women:

Older women likewise are to be reverent in their behavior, not malicious gossips, nor enslaved to much wine, teaching what is good, that they may encourage the young women to love their husbands, to love their children, to be sensible, pure, workers at home, kind, being subject to their own husbands, that the word of God may not be dishonored. (Titus 2:3-5)

Personally, I think we women tend to do too many

things outside the home. I know when I get too busy I have no energy left over to be all that I want to be for Chuck. I think this is particularly true of young mothers who have to work, or choose to work.

This Scripture gives us a list of things God wants women to be. He wants us to love our husbands and our children, to be sensible, pure, workers at home, to be kind, and to be subject to our own husbands. Why? So that the Word of God won't be dishonored. God says, "You can do it!" But we are so busy it takes all our energy just to survive. We haven't enough energy or time to get everything done that's expected of us. We become self-centered instead of self-controlled. We say things like, "I'm so tired and no one cares. I don't get any help around here. No one cares about *me*. My husband can just forget it—the kids can too!" This is when the Word of God is "dishonored," or "blasphemed," as another translation puts it. Women start thinking (and eventually saying out loud), "This marriage isn't working. How much does God want to put me through? Maybe everybody else is right. I should just go out and do my own thing, and let the rest of the family take care of themselves!"

God never told us to be busy. He said to love our husband and love our children with this love of affection and fun. It's our own fault that we get so burned out. Then we blame God and His name is dishonored. If we would just walk in the parameters and guidelines God has given us, it would be so much easier.

The time I feel most confused is when I have too much to do—when I feel time pressures and am overcommitted outside the home. Chuck and I find ourselves doing this too often, but I think I feel the pressure more than Chuck because my personality is tied up in how my home looks and whether everything is in order. I know Chuck has lots of pressure at his work too, but he can come home and take a nap or go out to his work shop and not even see the things I see that have to be done. He doesn't even know what to look for, so this is not meant to be a putdown to him. It's just the way things are. When I don't have enough time to do everything, I feel edgy and resentful and don't have the energy to be fun and flirty with Chuck.

I wish every husband could understand what he is missing when he insists that his wife go out to work. Even more, I wish young mothers would understand this too. God asks mothers to love their children in the same way they are to love their husbands—to be there for them, to make them feel special, to play with them, and to be everything they need.

Both the husband and wife are responsible to meet the other's needs. A man is told to nourish and cherish his wife. That word "nourish" means to bring to full maturity. "Cherish" means to create a warm atmosphere in which the wife can be brought to full maturity. When young people get married today, our culture seems to be asking the *wife* to bring her husband to full maturity by paying his way through school and working until he can get established in his career. We feel this is the opposite of what the Bible teaches.

Those of you who wear soft contacts know they have to be kept in the right atmosphere to be usable. If they are not, they dry up and get brittle like a cornflake. Then they can't do the job for which they were created. It's this same way with a wife. If the husband is not creating the right atmosphere for her growth, she will become sad, or angry, or unhappy, or resentful, and will not be the wife the man thought that he had married.

We once heard author and speaker Howard Hendricks tell about a man who came to him and complained how terrible his wife was. Howard asked him if she was like that when they got married. "Oh no," he said, "she was beautiful, wonderful, kind, and loving—just perfect for me." Howard said, "You mean you created THAT?" He had not created the right atmosphere for his wife's growth. In fact, he tore her down instead of building her up.

We mentioned that a man is told to nourish and cherish his wife as he would his own body. When you see everything a man is supposed to do as the head, it adds up to a big responsibility. The Lord says that in order for the man to be in headship, he needs to provide for his wife, to protect her, to be her servant-leader, to love her unconditionally, and to nourish and cherish her. That's a big job!

On the other hand, the woman is told to reverence her husband. This word "reverence" means to have a wholesome fear of ever displeasing him. It is the same word used when the Bible tells us to reverence the Lord. As *The Amplified Bible* indicates, this word means she is to notice him, regard him, honor him, prefer him, defer to him, appreciate him, and venerate and esteem him—to praise, prize, adore, enjoy, love and admire him exceedingly.

When you reverence someone, Scripture says this reverence is to be a controlling motive in your life. All you do and all you are is tied up in that person. I want to be all Chuck wants me to be. He often asks me what my five- and ten-year goals are. I wrote them down once and they never change, because my goals have to do with my relationship to God, and my relationships with my husband, children, grandchildren, family, and friends. We always laugh when he asks me that question, because our goals are so different. Most of the time he's just teasing, but there is definitely a difference in our goals. His are usually "doing," and mine are "being." I have as a controlling motive of my life to reverence the Lord and to reverence Chuck. I haven't arrived yet, but I'm working on it every day. When we stay in the roles God has given us, we build up each other.

In order to build each other up, the man is told:

Husbands, love your wives, and do not be embittered against them. (Colossians 3:19).

This "being embittered" mentioned here is an active, deliberate approach on the part of the husband. It's refusing to pick up your things that are laying around the house. It's not being willing to go on a date—just the two of you—even though your wife hasn't been out of the house for two weeks without the kids. It's not fixing that leaky faucet or broken chair she's been asking about for six months, even though you've fixed things for the neighbors. It is ignoring her and her wishes. Every couple has a different list.

You could embitter your wife by not wearing the clothes she thinks are right for the occasion. Our son and daughter-in-law, Tim and Tammie, came to one of our seminars where we explained that a wife's self-esteem is involved in the way her husband looks. Tim had been wearing a greasy old pair of deck shoes, but that afternoon he went out and bought a brand new pair of white tennis shoes, just so Tammie would feel good. He calls them his "love" shoes. That's an example of not embittering your wife. Even his mother thought he looked better!

Or you can embitter your wife by coming home from work and watching the TV or reading the paper while your wife prepares dinner, bathes the kids, gets them ready for bed, and does the dishes. Then later when she is exhausted and barely sits down, you make little hints about going to bed with you early. But she feels too tired, and then you feel rejected, having no idea how much you have embittered your wife all evening.

The word for "embittering" in the Greek means pricking, or putting a knife in and twisting it. It hurts terribly, and it's anything but unconditional love, dying to yourself, or nourishing and cherishing. It is being selfish and living for yourself only.

To avoid embittering his wife, a man is told to live in understanding with her.

You husbands likewise, live with your wives in an understanding way, as with a weaker vessel, since she is a woman; and grant her honor as a fellow-heir of the grace of life, so that your prayers may not be hindered. (1 Peter 3:7)

Living in understanding also means living according to knowledge. Each husband has a unique wife with her own personality and ways of doing things. What are those ways? What are her needs? How does she like things? Did you ever suspect that if you didn't live in understanding, your prayers would go unanswered? It makes sense because disregarding God's commands is sin. Why would He honor someone who is not obeying?

The wife needs a true leader—one who does not put himself first, but leads by serving. She needs to be loved unconditionally just as the husband loves his own body. She needs to be provided for and protected. She needs to be nourished and cherished. She needs her husband to avoid becoming embittered against her.

She also needs him to wash her with the Word—

...that He might sanctify her, having cleansed her by the washing of water with the word. (Ephesians 5:26)

The wife needs her husband to be in the Word so they can talk about the Lord together. When Chuck and I were young, we could never talk about the Lord without getting into an argument. I didn't understand what was happening, but I think I do now. At the time I was just beginning to study the Bible. I was learning faster than Chuck was, and I think it threatened him. In his heart he knew he should be learning too, but he just didn't have the motivation. When he did commit himself a hundred percent to the Lord, he too started growing and learning. The arguments stopped. We started sharing the Lord rather than making Him a battleground. I love to talk about Scripture with Chuck. We probably will never agree on everything but we are able to give our viewpoints to each other without conflict.

When Chuck is in the Word, I have confidence that he is going to make right decisions and pursue right actions. I know I can trust him, because he is getting guidance straight from the Lord. It is so much easier to submit to someone who is following the Lord and not his own impulses.

I really think a lot of the resistance that husbands feel from wives is because the wife is not sure her husband is hearing from the Lord. She never sees him in the Scriptures. I know Chuck is in the Scriptures. He has a Bible in every bathroom. He has a Bible with him in the car. When he goes to a counseling breakfast early in the morning, he takes his Bible so that if they don't show up, he has time to read. He talks about what he has been reading. We're both washed when he is in the Word.

Scripture also teaches that the woman is to be chaste in behavior, with a meek and quiet spirit, with her hope in God and not in her husband:

In the same way, you wives be submissive to your own hus-
bands so that even if any of them are disobedient to the
word, they may be won without a word by the behavior of
their wives, as they observe your chaste and respectful be-
havior. And let not your adornment be merely external
—braiding the hair, and wearing gold jewelry, and putting
on dresses; but let it be the hidden person of the heart, with
the imperishable quality of a gentle and quiet spirit, which
is precious in the sight of God. For in this way in former
times the holy women also, who hoped in God, used to
adorn themselves, being submissive to their own husbands.
Thus Sarah obeyed Abraham, calling him lord, and you
have become her children if you do what is right without
being frightened by any fear. (1 Peter 3:1-6)

Once again we see that wives are to be submissive
to their *own* husbands. And since some husbands are
not going to be in the Word to find out what it says,
wives are told to be submissive even if their husbands
are disobedient to the Word. The way a wife is to be
submissive is by her actions. For Scripture goes on to
say that our husbands can be won by our respectful
and chaste *behavior.* Again, that means having a wholesome dread of ever displeasing him.

Therefore you build him up, you admire him, you
defer to him, you praise him, you appreciate him, you
prize, adore, and enjoy him. All this for husbands who
do not obey the Lord. You see, it doesn't matter if your
husband is a Christian or not; he is yours, and God's
directions to you are clear. The rules don't change,
even though at times your husband may not be hearing God.

Chaste means to be physically pure and morally
righteous. No matter what our husbands do, we
remain physically true to them.

The reason we can keep our mouths closed and be

respectful and morally righteous is because we have that quality of meekness and quietness that is so becoming to a wife. We've mentioned that meekness is really strength under control. It is having a serenity of spirit because we know God rules over all. We know nothing can come into our lives unless God allows it. The Greek word for this was used to describe a cooling, soothing breeze.

The Greek word translated "quiet" means "to keep your seat." You know us women. We get excited and jump up and start talking rapidly. Well, this verse is saying to do just the opposite.

We can be calm and "seated" because our hope is in God. We don't have to depend on outward circumstances to control our inward state. We can be peaceful and serene no matter what, because our hope is in God. We know this is an inward quality, because the Lord says, "Let it be the hidden person of the heart." The Lord gives us Sarah's example of a meek and quiet spirit. Even when Abraham told Sarah to pretend she was his sister, and it led to her being taken into the harem of the ruler of the land through which they were passing, Sarah did as she was told and waited for God to protect and rescue her, which is exactly what God did. Through a dream He told the ruler that Sarah was really Abraham's wife. The ruler let her go immediately, and even bawled out Abraham for not telling him the truth.

I think we need to put our trust in the Lord more instead of always working out our own problems. If we would just keep quiet and know that God is God and let Him take over, we would walk in that meek and quiet spirit.

The man is to walk in meekness too. I say this because meekness is a fruit of the spirit. Also, Jesus says in Matthew 5 that the meek are blessed. All Christians need to be meek. We need to recognize that all things work together for good, because God is in control.

We all say hurtful things to each other at times. And probably the reason we're hurt is because there is some truth in what has been said about us. Sometimes communication is hard when one partner says hurtful words, but when we walk in meekness, it doesn't matter what is said. Our response should be to acknowledge that God has allowed this, and then to ask, "What truth is there in it? Is there anything He wants me to learn from this? How does He want me to change? Do I have a blind spot He is trying to point out?"

We can walk in meekness because we know God loves us and wants only our good. Sometimes what He brings into our life causes us hurt and discomfort, but we become more usable for the Lord when we change for the better.

The Greek word for meekness is also used in describing a stallion under control, prepared for his master's use. A horse has great power, but if it isn't under control, that power is useless. This is why the Lord spends so much time on us. He wants to mold us into His image, and make us usable.

Scripture goes on to remind us that the husband and wife are co-heirs:

You husbands likewise, live with your wives in an understanding way, as with a weaker vessel, since she is a woman; and grant her honor as a fellow-heir of the grace of life, so that your prayers may not be hindered. (1 Peter 3:7)

In the body of Christ, no one is above another. We are all equal. It is the same in a marriage. We do not have a hierarchy. We are in this together. We do have different roles, but one is not inferior to the other; they're just different.

In the body of Christ, no one is above another. We are all equal. It is the same in a marriage. We do not have a hierarchy. We are in this together. We do have different roles, but one is not inferior to the other; they're just different.

Another Scripture seems to contradict this principle of there being no hierarchy:

Let a woman quietly receive instruction with entire submissiveness. But I do not allow a woman to teach or exercise authority over a man, but to remain quiet. (1 Timothy 2:11-12)

I believe these verses speak to the husband-wife relationship and not to all men and women, both married and unmarried. The Greek words translated here as "woman" and "man" (they are in the singular—*A* man and *A* woman) can also be translated "wife" and "husband." In fact, these same Greek words are translated "husband" and "wife" in verse two of the following chapter in this same letter from Paul.

The Greek word translated "quiet" is the same word we discussed while looking at 1 Peter 3:4 (the one meaning "to keep your seat"). It does not mean a wife cannot speak. She is just to speak with the gentleness and quiet spirit that is becoming to a woman.

The Greek words for "teach" and "exercise authority" are in the present tense form which implies a continuous habit of life—something that is done over and over again. This would be illustrated by a wife who habitually takes the teaching or authority role in the marriage. Such a wife would be usurping her husband's position.

The Greek word for "exercise authority" refers to "self-starting authority." It does not mean a wife can never have authority, but rather that she should not assume that authority on her own. I would never make a decision that Chuck was against. I would never go ahead of him. If we are both serving one another, neither of us will do what the other is against.

The next point is the most important in our discussion: A Greek scholar has indicated to me that the last three words in the sentence, "I do not allow a woman to teach or exercise authority over a man" can be better translated "over *her* man," because they are in the genitive singular. We know from Ephesians 5:22 that wives are supposed to be submissive to their *own* husbands. If 1 Timothy 2:12 is interpreted to mean that I am to be in submission to *every* man, then we're forcing Scripture to contradict itself, which cannot be. I cannot be submissive to my own husband if I must also be submissive to every other man.

One of the principles of sound Bible interpretation is that Scripture interprets itself, and cannot contradict itself. If 1 Timothy 2:11-12 is interpreted to mean a woman must be in subjection to all men, no other Scripture backs it up—it just hangs alone. Therefore, Chuck and I believe this passage is teaching the same concepts that are taught in other Scripture passages that talk about the marriage role, such as Ephesians 5, 1 Peter 3, and Colossians 3. Husbands and wives really are fellow-heirs of the grace of life.

Man is the glory of God, and woman is the glory of a man:

But I want you to understand that Christ is the head of every man, and the man is the head of a woman, and God is the head of Christ...a man is the image and glory of God; but the woman is the glory of man. (1 Corinthians 11:3,7)

We have talked about how Christ is our example. God was Christ's example. Christ said He did only those things He saw His Father doing. That's where usage is singular. It is not men over women, but *A* man is the head of *A* woman.

One day I was listening to a portion of the Bible on tape, and heard these words—

Husbands, love your wives, just as Christ also loved the church and gave Himself up for her; that He might sanctify her, having cleansed her by the washing of water with the word, that He might present to Himself the church in all her glory, having no spot or wrinkle or any such thing; but that she should be holy and blameless. (Ephesians 5:25-27)

The word "glory" caught my attention. Christ was presenting the Church to Himself in all her glory. This means a husband should present to himself his *wife* in all her glory. What could this mean? I thought immediately of 1 Corinthians 11, where Paul says a woman is the glory of a man. "Glory" in its biblical usage means an opinion (always a good opinion in the New Testament), a correct estimate of, or praise and honor. Webster's includes this in defining "glory":

1. A great honor and admiration won by doing something important or valuable. Anything that brings fame and honor.

2. Worshipful adoration or praise.

3. The condition of highest achievement, splendor, and prosperity.

Then I thought of the woman in Proverbs 31 and all her achievements—how well her house was run, how well her husband and children were cared for, and how all her businesses were prospering. Verse 23 in this chapter reads:

Her husband is known in the gates, when he sits among the elders of the land.

This man had let his wife be all that she was meant to be. He let her do all that she did. As a result, not only did *she* receive honor for her accomplishments, but *he* did as well. He would not have received that honor unless he had created the atmosphere in which she could grow. She reflected glory back to him.

Then I thought of the description of Christ in Hebrews 1:3—

And He is the radiance of His (God's) *glory and the exact representation of His nature.*

Christ reflects back to God exactly what God is. Man is supposed to reflect back to Christ exactly what Christ is. And a woman is supposed to reflect back to her husband exactly what he is. When a person treats another in a Christlike way, they receive a reflection back of what we are to them. So, a man presents to himself his wife, just as Christ presents to Himself the Church in all her glory.

Some men present to themselves a contented wife; some men present to themselves a discontented wife. I have even heard of a husband who said to his wife, whom he had been neglecting, "If you'll just get happy, we'll do something this weekend!" But when a husband does something that deserves honor and praise, I believe the wife will reflect that back to him.

Are we presenting to ourselves the kind of relationship that is honoring to God, or dishonoring? Is it honoring to ourselves, or dishonoring?

To honor each other, the husband and wife cannot be independent from each other:

However, in the Lord, neither is woman independent of man, nor is man independent of woman. (1 Corinthians 11:11)

This fits so well with servant-leadership and servant-submission. It fits the example given to us by the relationship of God and Christ. Neither God nor Christ makes independent decisions. It also fits the principle of being fellow-heirs together of the grace of life. If we are to honor each other, we cannot and must not make independent decisions. When anyone enters a covenant relationship, they watch out for the interests of the other person.

In marriage we are in a covenant. In the body of Christ we are in a covenant. We should always be putting the interests of others before our own. We are not independent in any relationship, and especially in marriage. Since marriage is a picture of our relationship with Christ, we never do anything unless we first ask ourselves: Is this what the Lord wants me to do?

How do we know if we are being submissive? Two passages of Scriptures give special help us on this:

For you have been called for this purpose, since Christ also suffered for you, leaving you an example for you to follow in His steps, who committed no sin, nor was any deceit found in His mouth, and while being reviled, He did not revile in return; while suffering, He uttered no threats, but kept entrusting Himself to Him who judges righteously; and He Himself bore our sins in His body on the cross, that we might die to sin and live to righteousness; for by His wounds you were healed. For you were continually straying like sheep, but now you have returned to the Shepherd and Guardian of your souls. (1 Peter 2:21-25)

Therefore, since Christ has suffered in the flesh, arm yourselves also with the same purpose, because he who has suffered in the flesh has ceased from sin, so as to live the rest of the time in the flesh no longer for the lusts of men, but for the will of God. (1 Peter 4:1-2)

Our purpose in life should be to please God by following the example Christ left for us, as Scripture tells us to do. In 1 Peter 3 we read, *"In the same way* you wives..." and "You husbands *likewise..."* These two phrases refer back to the description in chapter 2 of the exemplary attitude the Lord demonstrated for us when He was suffering unjustly.

- He committed no sin.
- No deceit was found in His mouth.
- While being reviled, He did not revile in return.
- While suffering, He did not threaten.
- He kept entrusting Himself to God because He knew that God judges righteously.
- He bore our sins in His own body.
- Because he was willing to bear our sins, He healed our wounds.

When it says there was no deceit in Christ's mouth, it means He didn't say one thing and mean another. He didn't do anything underhandedly, secretly, or insidiously.

It would be like going out and buying a blouse that you know you can't afford, then keeping it under wraps for two or three weeks—so that when your husband asks, "Is that new?," you say, "I've had it for weeks." Or for a husband to say he is just too tired to finish painting the bedroom, as he has promised to do for weeks, when in reality he just doesn't want to do it today.

One of my friends told me that when she was young and had a disagreement with her husband, she would always fix him tuna-fish casserole for dinner and then tell him that was all they could afford. But she really prepared it because she knew he did not like tuna-fish casserole.

Or, it may be telling your partner everything is okay when all you really want to do is avoid a conflict.

If you do things like this, you are not being submissive to each other.

The word "revile" means open abuse. When the Lord was openly abused, He did not openly abuse in return. He didn't return evil for evil, nor did he threaten. He didn't say, "You'll be sorry some day. Just wait until you see what I'm going to do to you!" It's the same when a marriage partner says, "I'm going to divorce you if you ever do that again." It's openly abusing and threatening. If you find yourself saying things like this, you are not being submissive.

The Lord prayed about the situation in which He found Himself. He kept entrusting Himself to God, who judges righteously. He could do this because He knew He had done no wrong. He knew He was doing the will of the Father, and God is pleased when we obey Him even when we're falsely accused. Scripture says, "And call upon Me in the day of trouble; I shall rescue you, and you will honor Me." Jesus knew God would be true to His Word.

Another thing the Lord did was to bear our sins in His body, so that we are spiritually healed. Are we willing to forget all the bad things our mates have done to us even though they don't even recognize what they've done? Can we give them kindness and healing? If a wife keeps her mouth shut and doesn't even say a word, it's a form of bearing another person's sin. Or when a husband lives in understanding with his wife, even though he doesn't like it, he is bearing her sins in his own body. He can do this because he knows God judges righteously.

And further, we can be submissive in spite of ill treatment because we have armed ourselves with the same purpose with which Christ armed Himself. We have decided not to live the rest of our life in the flesh for the lusts of men, but for the will of God.

So this is how you will know if you are being submissive:

- You do no wrong.
- You don't deceive, or openly abuse.
- You don't return evil for evil.
- You don't threaten.
- You keep praying.
- You trust God to judge righteously.
- You keep your mouth shut.
- You live in understanding.
- You decide not to live for yourself.
- You live for the will of God.

These decisions have to be made before the conflicts come. We need to realize again that it isn't God's harshness that wins us, but rather His kindness. It isn't our harshness that will win others either. It will be our kindness and our obedience to God.

I guess the bottom line for me was learning from the Bible how God expected me to treat Barb, and then trying to do it right. If you're fighting our view of mutual submission, or the concept of headship not meaning decision making, or the value of dying and serving your wife, check out Scripture for yourself and see if you don't come to the same conclusion.

This is a hard message for men especially, because so many of our churches are doing a poor job presenting the balance in the relationship between a husband and wife. But if you are a true Christian, having asked Jesus Christ to come in and take control of your life and to make you be the person He wants you to be, then you have the power to change. If you and your partner are not Christians, you can change for a few weeks, but usually the relationship deteriorates back to where it was because neither partner has the supernatural power to do the right thing regardless of how they feel. Love is action, not feelings. We are to be ministers to each other. We are to focus on each other's needs. There will be good feelings for sure, but they'll come *after* doing the right thing, and not before.

13

How Grows Your Garden?

(BARB:) We spoke earlier about husbands nourishing and cherishing their wives. Remember that "nourish" means to bring to full maturity, and "cherish" means to create a warm atmosphere. This is where we get the principle of the man being in charge of the atmosphere of the home. It is the idea of brooding as a hen does for her chicks, keeping them at just the right temperature so they might be brought to full maturity. The Lord said in Matthew 23:37-38:

"O Jerusalem, Jerusalem, who kills the prophets and stones those who are sent to her! How often I wanted to gather your children together, the way a hen gathers her chicks under her wings, and you were unwilling. Behold your house is being left to you desolate!"

Jesus is speaking of Jerusalem here, but I think of this as a graphic picture of wives who are not being brooded.They are desolate. It's not something we can turn off and on easily. Remember the husband who said they would go away for the weekend if she would just get *happy*? She was only reflecting what she was getting from him.

(CHUCK:) Gary Smalley uses the example of the husband as a gardener. The bad gardener goes into the garden and bawls out the beans for being a little brown, or the carrots for wilting, or the tomatos for getting rotten—yet he will not provide the right kind of fertilizer or the water or the tender loving care the garden needs. The good gardener examines his garden, lives in understanding with it, provides the warm atmosphere and materials needed to bring it to full maturity—just as a husband is to do for his wife. If wives don't get the things they need, they close up like a rhododendron bud. If we nourish and cherish our wives like the Bible tells us to, then they can grow and blossom and bloom and get perfume all over us. They radiate back to us exactly what we are giving them. If you see a happy wife, you can assume the husband is doing a good job nourishing and cherishing. If you see a sad wife, you can bet the husband is failing in the nourishing and cherishing department.

I went to a Christian management seminar once and the man up front was talking about how he and his wife were teammates in the ministry together, and how much they thought alike and had similar priorities. His wife, however, was sitting over in the corner as far away from him as she could—all shriveled up like a prune, with a pinched face and folded arms.

This is not to say a woman doesn't have any responsibility to grow spiritually on her own. Both partners are responsible before God to learn how to grow in living a life of godliness and holiness and love. The man just has an extra role, which is creating the atmosphere for his wife's growth.

But things get complicated when a wife tries to be her

husband's Holy Spirit: "Why aren't you in the Word?" "How can you go hunting on Sunday morning and miss church?" "When will we ever start praying together?" If a man is pressed too much, he often will just back away and ignore what she is saying.

One of our pastor friends, Ken Hutcherson, says the wife has to duck so God can "smash" the husband. If the wife is part of the problem, then the husband resists her and God doesn't stand much of a chance, humanly speaking. If she starts being the woman God wants her to be, then the man is resisting only God—and God has effective ways of dealing one-on-one with wayward kids.

Once we spoke at a women's retreat, and then a few weeks later spoke to many of their husbands at a men's retreat. Our message to each group was a bit different. We urged the women to be godly wives in spite of their husbands' failures. To the men we spoke about dying for their wives, serving them, and valuing them as a "10." We were told that during the week after the men's retreat, one husband got up in front of the whole congregation and said he had been a jerk for twenty-five years of marriage, and that God had gotten his attention on this issue because his wife had begun "anointing his feet." In other words, she had ceased being part of the problem.

On the other hand, I see nothing in Scripture advising the wife to stick around the house when she is getting beat up every night. If there is physical abuse involved, she probably needs to remove herself from the situation, and maybe by doing that she will get her husband's attention and he will seek help. We are not asked to be doormats, but when a wife is able to carry out her role as a godly woman regardless of what her husband does, we have seen some amazing turnarounds in the husband's attitude and behavior.

James Dobson's book *Love Must Be Tough* is must reading on the topic of abusive relationships. But a word of caution applies with every book you read—even ours. Don't try to take every word as God's gospel to you. Some things apply, some don't. There are unique circumstances in every life. But in the best books the bottom line message usually comes out loud and clear and with broad application, and this is surely the case with Dr. Dobson's book.

One practical way a husband can nourish and cherish his wife is by helping her recognize her spiritual gift. Maybe she has the gift of mercy and could volunteer as a helper in a hospital or rest home. Or perhaps she has the gift of helps and can serve on a social or service committee at church. Or if she has the gift of administration, she can be a deaconess or serve on the Christian Education Board. We feel many women have the gift of pastor-shepherd and can lead Bible studies and do counseling. The Bible states clearly that a woman cannot fill the POSITION of a Pastor or Elder, because that person has to be the husband of one wife, and that's a little hard for a woman to do. But even though she isn't to fill the position, she can easily have that spiritual gift, and work with a group of "sheep." I'm sure Barb has this shepherding gift, among others.

The wife might have a speaking gift of some kind. Some husbands get threatened by having their wife up front teaching while their gift is serving or helping in the background. But the rules don't change. As the husband he is still to provide the atmosphere and opportunity for her to exercise her gift.

I'd love to preach the Word like Chuck Swindoll. Or write and sing music like the Gaithers. Or bring thousands of people to Christ like Billy Graham. I don't have those gifts. We need to be careful not to look at other people and try to copy their gifts which we may or may not have. We need to be who WE are, with our own unique gifts and area of ministry. Those of us in business will probably have lunch or breakfast with hundreds of people who would not be caught dead viewing Billy Graham on TV, or listening to a Chuck Swindoll tape, or tapping their foot to Gaither music, or going to church. You might be the only "Christ" they will ever see, and only you can reach these people for Christ.

A husband should also help his wife with nonspiritual gifts. If she likes to sew, he should make sure she has a good sewing machine. If she is a budding artist, he should let her take art lessons and provide the brushes and paints.

I like to try new things all the time, and some years ago I took some art lessons at our local YWCA. I had a great time, but made the mistake of leaving my paints and brushes out one night. Barb tried them the next day, and while my pictures resemble the work of Grandma Moses, hers look more like Rembrandt or Norman Rockwell. Many of the pictures hanging in our home were painted by her.

I think we've mentioned that Barb and I have different spiritual gifts. Her main gift is that of a teacher, and she loves to spend hours at a time getting into the Bible, doing word studies, examining the tenses and sentence structure in a passage. My principal gift is one of exhortation. That means I like to come alongside someone and help him put Scripture into shoe leather. I realize not all of you will agree (Barb included), but I get excited with ANY sign of growth. It's a process. I can easily say to my brand new Christian friend, "You're down from five angry outbursts at your kids every week to just three. Praise the Lord, that's TERRIFIC! Keep up the good work!" And pretty soon he'll have forgotten how to yell.

If a couple is brand new in the Lord, I don't expect them to immediately throw off every worldly aspect in their lifestyle. They have to see for themselves where they are wrong, and this takes someone gently and tenderly leading them into a personal understanding from Scripture about what God's desires are. There's a balance here, of course— we don't want to keep giving praise to wheel-spinners—but I think sometimes we expect new believers to be mind-readers and to know Scripture back and forth when they can barely find Genesis.

As I mentioned, Barb spends hours at a time studying the Bible. I spend minutes at a time in bathrooms, before appointments, and in waiting rooms and cars. Neither of us is wrong in our pattern—we're just different.

The key to nourishing our wives is to make them our highest priority—higher on our list than sports, TV, hunting, camping, work, and even ministry. I see some pastors and teachers who violate this principle by saying, in effect, "Lord, you take care of the family, and I'll take care of the sheep." You're not even supposed to give a man a position in the church until his family is in order. Scripture makes this clear:

Before they are asked to be deacons, they should be given other jobs in the church as a test of their character and ability, and if they do well, then they may be chosen as deacons. Their wives must be thoughtful, not heavy drinkers, not gossipers, but faithful in everything they do. Deacons should have only one wife and they should have happy, obedient families. (1 Timothy 3:10-12)

We feel the biblical priorities for a man are first his relationship with Christ, then his wife, then his kids. Then he is to provide for his family. Then, if he has time, he can have a ministry. I've met people in full-time ministry whose families were on welfare because the father wasn't providing for them adequately. Often what God is telling a person like that is, "GO GET A JOB," but somehow they are deaf to that. After you have provided for your family and have a little time left over, then you can be a youth leader, or camp counselor, or minister with a group like Campus Crusade. I believe this ranking of priorities isn't MY list, but rather God's, reflecting what He has written in His Word about priorities.

If we men put our wives first after our relationship with Christ, this means we won't always get our way. Christ didn't always get His way, and He is our example in this. We might not go hunting or fishing as often as we would like, or watch TV as much as we want. We might have to go to more funerals, anniversaries, and weddings than we feel our systems can tolerate.

It even means letting our wife have the fuzzy toilet seat-cover that prevents the lid from staying up. I hate those things. Fortunately they have not been a big deal with Barb, but I find them in the homes of many of our friends. I don't think women know how hard it is to balance yourself there with one foot holding up the lid. It's just plain awkward.

By the way, I think men are getting a bad rap on this toilet seat bit. We get all sorts of flak when we don't put them down, but have our wives ever thought of leaving them UP for us? It seems that in this culture of equality it takes no more energy to put the lid up than it does to put it down. But maybe this is just part of a husband dying for his wife.

We can show our wives how important they are to us by bringing them flowers. But don't get a potted plant that will last twenty years. Get her a delicate bud that will last only a half hour. This says to her, "You're so important to me I blew some of my money on this flower that will be wilted in no time."

Give her love gifts for no reason. Put it on your calendar if you need a reminder. Once in a while I will stop by the magazine rack at Safeway and pick up six or eight women's magazines and leave them on Barb's desk as a surprise. Make sure you remember her birthday, Valentine's Day, and your wedding anniversary without needing hints. Again, put those important dates on your calendar. It's rude and thoughtless to forget. I have a "tickler" file where I have folders for each day of the month and each month of the year. If something is coming up in the future, I just put a note in the appropriate folder and I don't have to worry about remembering it.

In January, I buy as many cards as I can for the whole year—for her birthday, our anniversary, Valentine's Day, etc.. I put them in the file to pop up a few days before I need them. I grieve at the number of wives being made into dried prunes because of uncaring, insensitive husbands who always need prodding to remember important dates— men who are self-centered, who hardly ever take time to talk, who never resolve marriage conflicts, who never follow their wife's counsel, and who in fact treat the dog better than they do her.

Part of nourishing and cherishing involves the husband paying a price for his wife. If, in fact, I love Barb as Christ loved the church, then she can't weigh too much, spend too much time on the phone, talk to her mother too much, watch too much TV, etc. If any of these things alters my love for her, then I have conditional love, not the unconditional love Christ has for me and asks me to have for my wife. That doesn't mean a man has to be doormat or a milquetoast. It just means he should put her needs first. When he does that, she responds and looks to him for leadership and meets his needs.

BARB: At one of our conferences a woman raised her hand and said it sounded like Chuck had done all the changing in our relationship. I knew I had changed a lot too, but it was hard to think on my feet, so I didn't give a very good answer. Later a friend came up to me and asked, "Don't you know how you've changed, Barb?" She then reminded me of all the projects with which Chuck had involved me, like speaking engagements, putting in a pickleball court at our home, and ministries like being chaplains for the University of Washington football team, co-teaching the Mariner baseball couples' Bible study, participating with the Seahawks at their couple's Bible study, traveling and teaching at retreats, serving on the national staff of Pro Athlete's Outreach, and so on. She helped me see that I had changed in the areas of ministry goals and personal development, while Chuck had changed in the relationship area.

I've also changed by trying to honor Chuck and cook the things he likes. If I had my way, there would be some all-vegetable dinners and not so much meat. He also loves the same thing over and over again, and doesn't like many of the things I do. I'll compromise by adding some things to the meal for me, but I also make sure I have what he likes too. Once in a while I'll remind him how much he hates to do the same thing over and over again, and that's how I feel about cooking the same meals all the time.

I'm a perfectionist when it comes to keeping the house clean. But I have compromised for a couple of "his" areas in the house. He can keep them like he wants (messy), but before company comes he picks them up and makes them presentable. We don't even talk about it anymore. He just cleans his areas automatically when we have people coming over.

In our other home we had a dining room table that Chuck called the "Bermuda Triangle." It was one of the first things you saw when you entered the front door, and the family kept putting things on it when they came home from school or work.

CHUCK: Hold it! Now what's the use of having a dining room table if you can't put things on it? Somehow the things the family put on the table would disappear. We used to have four kids, now we have just three because one of the kids sat on her table and hasn't been seen since. I sat my briefcase on it one time, and it also went poof! I panicked because all my "brains" were in there, but Barb somehow summoned its return after some anxious moments.

BARB: Well, it just wasn't "me" to have the dining room table messy. I have, however, given in as far as

Chuck's home office is concerned in our present home. He is trying to make it into a Smithsonian museum. He has cameras and recorders and film and papers all over the place. I used to give him a bad time, but I've changed and now just ask that he close his rolltop desk and clear the floor when we have company. I don't dare look into the closet. When we don't have guests I just let him be who he wants to be in his office. He is comfortable with things in what I would call disorder.

Part of this has to do with his personality style. Chuck was born with high energy, and is almost a pure choleric. This means he likes to keep doing things, not just sitting or standing around. However, when Chuck learned that people are eternal but things and projects are only temporal, his whole priority system changed.

I was his secretary during the time he was learning this. He had an appointment to counsel someone. The person went into his office and talked and talked. I got very nervous thinking Chuck would be upset because he had so many deadlines that day. After the person left I noticed Chuck was as relaxed as he was when the day began. I asked him about it, and he said counseling was much more important than getting his commercials written. He could always write at night, but he couldn't always be there when someone was hurting. He's operated on that principle ever since.

CHUCK: When a husband is being insensitive in a certain area, one of the best clues is not only a disheartened wife, but a wife who keeps bringing up the same subject over and over again. During our hard times we would have a conflict and Barb would bring up one of the instances where I had failed her or lost money in a deal that she was against, and my response would be, "I thought we talked about that. Why are you bringing that up again?" She was bringing it up because she didn't think I knew how she really felt. I knew most of the facts surrounding the event, but had missed most or all of the emotional messages Barb was sending.

Again Gary Smalley came to my rescue and suggested we open up each other's spirit. We do this by making a list of the ways we KNOW we have offended our mate. We don't have to use the word "if." When you use "if" it really means, "If I have hurt you (but I don't think I did), then please forgive me." You usually know very well what you did, so make a list and take her out to a quiet restaurant and ask for her forgiveness for those things—like tempting her sexually before you were married, not helping her with the kids enough when they were young, not taking her counsel and losing money on investments, spending too much time at work or play that took away from time with her.

After you get through your list, ask her whether she can remember any other times you've hurt her. (She can remember what you wore on your first date, and whether you put ketchup on your hamburger that night.) Often during this forgiveness process she can come up with something you have forgotten: "The time you got angry in front of my folks and stomped out of the house." Respond by saying, "I didn't even remember that—please forgive me for being so insensitive and unloving." This might seem "false" to a man, but he needs to fight through that feeling and take care of everything—even those things he has forgotten. The wife will be grateful he cares enough to do this.

The wife can also have a list, and she, too, should ask her husband's forgiveness.

Barb and I did this, and I can truthfully tell you she has not brought up one of the things on my list again in a conflict situation. She remembers the facts, of course. She still feels badly about some of them, but she knows I know how she felt in the situation, so she doesn't have to keep bringing it up over and over.

Go through this same type of procedure with parents, with bosses, with neighbors, with people at church, and with your kids. The point is to ask forgiveness for the things YOU have done without worrying about anything others have done. You take care of your part, and let God put the pressure on them to take care of their part. In fact if they never ask your forgiveness, it should be okay as far as you are concerned. Just take care of your own house, and let God work in the other person's life the way He knows best.

I think it's interesting to reflect on our Lord's statement to the apostle Peter when he was asked how many times he should forgive someone. Evidently the Jewish rulers of the day said you had to forgive someone three times. Christ told Peter to forgive seventy times seven—490 times! I think the context is suggesting there is no end to forgiveness. Can you imagine keeping track for 490 times? Have you ever forgiven anyone three or even four times? If we would ever get to five times we would probably write them off.

We recommend that married couples have a weekly date if they are having lots of conflicts, or at least once a month if things are fairly calm. The whole purpose of the date is to talk about your relationship and whether you have hurt each other during the past week (month). The discussion takes place when emotions are calm and both can talk about the situations without much anger. You can leave the restaurant friends again.

It's really up to the man to initiate this procedure. He's not going to be real excited about doing this, because he is usually mostly at fault, and it's painful to have his failures pointed out. He must do this, however, because it's part of loving his wife as Christ loved the church and died for her. The feelings follow after the action is taken.

Consistency is another key. Don't let one person unilaterally determine everything is going well so you won't have to have your date this month. Chances are the other person is "screaming," and they are not being heard. So make a covenant with each other to have your weekly / monthly date without fail. Put it on your calendar and don't let anything short of World War III keep you from that appointed time. It doesn't always have to be heavy. I'm sure there will be lots of times when you both agree that everything's fine. If so, enjoy the evening and talk about whatever comes to mind. What I'm trying to say is that there must be mutual agreement that nothing is wrong. One party does not have the right to determine this alone.

One of the great benefits of opening each other's spirit is feeling like you're almost beginning again at the dating stage. You are free and open in your heart toward each other. The past is past, and you can look forward to the future.

In Matthew 5:23, Jesus sets the principle for us:

"If therefore you are presenting your offering at the altar, and there remember that your brother (or sister) *has something against you, leave your offering there before the altar, and go your way; first be reconciled to your brother, and then come and present your offering."*

God is not interested in our sacrifices as much as He is in our obedience. If both husband and wife are Christians, the man should initiate the process. If only one partner is a Christian, then it is the one with the "light" that should take the first step in asking forgiveness and making things right. Then when we know we have a clear conscience, we can worship God with complete freedom, knowing we have His blessing.

I think God set up marriage as the perfect situation for all concerned. I laugh as I hear my feminist friends get all uptight about the Bible calling God a "Him." I suppose that's better than "it," but God had both male and female characteristics, as we have mentioned before. He gave different of His characteristics to Adam and Eve. He is not just male, or just female—He is both. Marriage brings these different characteristics together again.

First of all we have the man as the provider. He takes care of sheltering and feeding his family. He works hard out there in the cruel world. The woman creates a "nest" for him and the children. When he comes home from the battles, he enters a sanctuary built by the woman. She honors him, respects him, appreciates his care, builds him up, flirts with him, takes him to bed early, feeds him, ministers to him, and likes him a lot.

In return the man appreciates all this support and lovingly serves his wife and children, living in understanding with them so he can tell what they need to be brought to full maturity. The children are discipled with love, firmness, and fun. You'll notice I used the word "discipled." I'm sure many of you have had someone ask you to "disciple" them, which means to meet with them on a regular basis for Bible study and be involved in their lives as a counselor. Jesus Christ is our example of a good discipler. His attributes are tenderness, kindness, patience, gentleness, unconditional love, and forgiveness. The word "disciple" comes from the same root word as "discipline." Yet when a person thinks of discipline, words like spankings, harshness, abuse, conditional love, revenge, bitterness, and unforgiving spirit so often come to mind.

In God's plan the mother teaches the young girl how to "nest" and how to manage a home and how to care for and serve the family. The dad teaches the young boy how to stand up to the bullies and to honor his mom and to exercise self-control and to provide loving servant leadership at home. Each person in the family has a definite and distinct role that is invaluable and irreplaceable.

God's plan is hindered somewhat when young mothers work outside the home. Sometimes there is no choice, but sometimes the sacrifice of time and emotional energy is for nothing except to say she has a career, and she hopes people will applaud. God won't, but the misguided in our culture might. If that's fulfilling for her, I guess she will have to go on that, but it's a miserable substitute for the richness of a biblical marriage which is far beyond the imagination in its potential to meet the needs of husband, wife, father, mother and children. God's plan is hindered even more when dads neglect their precious families—or leave them altogether. We are in effect as bad as the heathen tribes who used to throw their babies into a volcano as sacrifices to their gods. Now the idols are called career, time, convenience, and self. It's exactly the same thing, only different idols.

Why is this so hard to see? Why must children suffer to prove the truth of God's way? Don't sacrifice your family on the altars of money and things and status and careers. Try it God's way. If you go ahead and do your own thing, you'll be missing the richest experience this life can offer.

14

Blue Shoes or Brown?

(CHUCK:) One of the mysteries of womanhood is the fact that a woman can be the president of IBM, make two million dollars a year, and be in constant demand on the lecture circuit, but still needs her husband's approval to feel good about herself. This can be confusing to men.

For instance, as you're preparing to go out together she might ask you, "Which shoes would you want me to wear—the blue ones or the brown ones?" (You look terrific in either one, Dear—you choose.) "No, which ones do you want me to wear, blue or brown?" (Mmmm, the blue pair.) "I think I'll wear the brown," announces the wife.

Barb and I like to go out to dinner, and just as we're pulling out the driveway I will ask her where she wants to go eat. (I don't care, where do YOU want to go?) "I don't care, where do you want to go?" (I don't care; what sounds good to you?) I'll then name a restaurant, and Barb will say something like "YUCK!"

If they don't want a decision from us, why do they ask? I'm told it's because they want to make sure we're part of their world. They already know what they want to do, but they want to see if we think they are important enough to be involved with them in decision making, even though they don't want our advice. Make sense? I didn't think so.

A man tends to make snap decisions, a woman is a little slower. The reason is that she is usually looking at all sides of the situation with her computer brain—checking out all the details, seeing if it will be practical and not blow the budget, or alienate all her friends, etc. The man is usually more impulsive. He's just looking at the goal. For instance, he finds a great bargain on a motor home and buys it. He might not have any place to park it, but he has saved lots of money on the deal. I think Barb mentioned my buying a set of exercise equipment that didn't fit in the basement. It looked great in the showroom, so I bought it. I didn't think to measure the basement.

This doesn't mean I'm suggesting the wife and husband check with each other on every little purchase. Just set a limit, and agree that for anything over that amount, the other person must be consulted first. If you're wondering what the amount should be, I propose, say, $10,000. (Barb would probably suggest $15. Just split the difference.)

Men tend to give quick solutions for problems. Women don't usually want solutions, they just want us to know how they feel in a certain situation. They want understanding. We had a painter working around our house. He was usually late for his appointments and always questioned Barb's colors. She tried to tell me how she felt one time, and I said, "Get rid of him—get someone else." But she liked his work, and didn't want to get rid of him. She just wanted me to know and acknowledge her feelings.

When she told me about the painter coming late, what I should have said was, "I'll bet that frustrates you, doesn't it? You don't know whether you can go shopping, start a project around the house, even get on the phone without being interrupted." When she told me about him criticizing her colors I should have said, "This is your home—and you have the right to choose any colors you want. In fact I love what you're doing." I might still think we should get rid of him, but all she wanted me to do was listen to her feelings without giving a bunch of solutions with three easy steps to get rid of her problem.

One of the things that got me in trouble early in our marriage was that I always thought understanding meant agreement. Since Barb and I are so different we seldom agree on anything, but I've found I can understand how she feels without having to agree with her.

We need to practice being active listeners—not just hearing, but listening with our eyes, heart and ears without glazing over or being distracted by something on TV or outside.

I went to a communication seminar once where I learned a practical exercise in listening. We were to choose from a list the subject we wanted to discuss with someone. There were lots of controversial things on the list, like abortion, nuclear disarmament, the feminist movement, AIDS, and that type of thing. After we selected our subject and found a partner, Person A was to present his ideas on the subject for two minutes. Person B could do nothing but listen. After the two minutes were over, Person B could ask questions concerning Person A's statement, but could not add any of her own ideas and comments. Person B kept asking questions until Person A confirmed that B had heard exactly what he had meant to say. Then for two minutes Person B stated her case, and all Person A could do was listen and later ask questions. An amazing thing happened. Maybe for the first time in their lives, people were hearing the other side of controversial issues. We tend to have our minds made up regardless of the facts, don't we? I even saw people switch sides after learning the other person's viewpoint.

When was the last time you listened two full minutes to your husband or wife without adding comments or making suggestions as to why they were off target? Try that same listening exercise sometime, maybe during your weekly communication date. You'll be amazed at what you learn.

We can do the same thing with our kids—be a mirror to their feelings. We don't have to agree with what they are feeling, but we need to acknowledge their right to feel any way they want—even angry feelings that so often threaten us. Just reflect the feelings back with statements like these: "You're really angry with us right now, aren't you?" "You really wanted to go the park, didn't you?" "That doll your friend broke meant a great deal to you, didn't it?" "You're upset that dinner is ready and you want to go outside, aren't you?" We don't have to get all tied up with their negative emotions. Let them feel them. Then reflect the feelings back to them, and they'll KNOW you understand. You can deal with the particulars later at a calmer time.

Again, in marriage men are usually the initiators, and women are the responders. Barb and I feel if a man does it right in a marriage relationship, the woman is almost powerless not to respond in a like matter. Sure there are times when there's so much background and baggage to stagger through it takes a while for the wife to believe her husband has really changed; but time does heal.

If there's continuing conflict in the relationship, it's the man who has to break the cycle of mutual criticism. He is the one who is to wash his wife with the Word and love her unconditionally, and then she will respond.

We have couples who come to us for counseling, and one or both will say, "I just don't love him (or her) anymore." Our sincere response is something like, "What difference does that make?" Love is not a feeling, but rather action. The feelings come AFTER the action. Are you doing good, kind, loving things for your mate? If you are, then you can be sure the feelings will come. The feelings are a consequence of loving action. Most of the time when someone doesn't feel love anymore, it's because of failing to do loving things. In fact, often he or she is hardly speaking to the other person.

I look at 1 Corinthians 13—which some people call the Love Chapter—as an example of this perspective. Part of this passage reads:

> *Love is patient.*
> *Love is kind.*
> *Love is never jealous.*
> *Love is never envious.*
> *Love is not boastful.*
> *Love is not proud.*
> *Love is not haughty.*
> *Love is not selfish.*
> *Love is not rude.*
> *Love does not demand its own way.*
> *Love is not irritable.*
> *Love is not touchy.*
> *Love does not hold grudges.*
> *Love doesn't notice when you do something wrong.*
> *Love is never glad about injustice.*
> *Love rejoices when truth wins.*
> *Love is loyal.*
> *Love believes in a person.*
> *Love expects the best from a person.*
> *Love defends a person.*

I don't know about you, but I don't find many things in that list that are only feelings. What I see most is things that involve doing. Scripture affirms that DOING is what counts:

Dear brothers, what's the use of saying that you have faith and are Christians if you aren't proving it by helping others? Will that kind of faith save anyone? If you have a friend who is in need of food and clothing, and you say to him, "Well good-bye,

and God bless you; stay warm and eat hearty," and then don't
give him clothes or food, what good does that do? So you see, it
isn't enough just to have faith. You must also do good to prove
that you have it. Faith that doesn't show itself by good works is
no faith at all—it is dead and useless. (James 2:14-17)

After we DO something, THEN God gives us the feelings to go with the action.

There is an additional requirement, however, to this love-is-action principle: It's having the right attitude.

At church one Sunday evening we were having a promotional program for summer camp. I had seen a camp program once, so why would I want to see another? They usually consist of 127 dark slides and 76 kids telling their experiences from last year. I have nothing against camps, and I love kids, but I'm not into camp programs at church, so I suggested Barb go without me. She pointed out—correctly, I might add—that she willingly went with me to some of the things I enjoyed, and she wanted me to go with her to the camp program which she knew she would enjoy. I really am selfish that way. She always has such a sweet spirit about going with me to my events, that I forget she comes just to be with me and not because she is thrilled with the activity.

But because I was being my old selfish self, my back started aching terribly. My head began to throb. My neck creaked. My legs got weak, my palms sweaty, and I'm afraid I made Barb's life miserable until we left the house.

We got to church, and sure enough the program was bad. In fact, it was much worse than I had thought possible. That made my back go into spasms. Finally it was over, and everything hit the fan on the way home. Barb did not like it that I had made her life miserable.

I didn't instantly know why I had behaved as I did, but the next day I called home from work and told her why my back had hurt so much. If I had gone with a smiley isn't-this-wonderful look on my face, then she would want to go AGAIN sometime, or stay an extra hour. If she was miserable I had half a chance of getting out of there at a decent hour. So we made a deal. I would go with a happy attitude the next time, but when she looked over and saw me smiling and laughing, she was to assume that I was MISERABLE and try to get me out of there as soon as she could.

She blew it not long after we had made that agreement. We went to a wedding. She saw me smiling, chatting, and having a good time, so she decided to stay another hour, even though I was anxious to get on with my life.

It's not that I don't love the people involved. I do. It's just that I can't become a success in life spending my sunset years at camp programs and weddings.

It really doesn't do much good to do something for your mate if you're going to have a crummy attitude. Love is action with a loving attitude. It's easy to just go on feelings. It's hard to do the right thing and stick with something. This is probably why so many marriages split up. Neither party is willing to do the good, kind things for the other, and they walk away from the relationship and go out and find someone else. Then four people have the problem rather than the original two (which explains why about seventy percent of second marriages fail, according to one report I've seen). It's only when we work THROUGH our problems that we become valuable to anyone else, as Scripture confirms:

Dear brothers, is your life full of difficulties and temptations? Then be happy, for when the way is rough, your patience has a chance to grow. So let it grow, and don't try to squirm out of your problems. For when your patience is finally in full bloom, then you will be ready for anything, strong in character, full and complete. (James 1:2-4)

I think the context is clear. We have to go THROUGH the problems to experience what God wants us to learn, and in that way have a message that will help other people go through the same thing.

So many of us fight against our circumstances, blaming God for not paying attention to our lives or not hearing our prayers. Or we blame our difficulties on our mate, our parents, our boss, our neighbor, or our church leaders. Personally, I'm sure I have stretched a certain trial to last a month when God meant it to be over in half that time. But after the first two weeks had gone by, I was still fighting my circumstances and asking God whether He was spending too much time in Ethiopia and not enough looking after me. God in effect had to prolong the difficult circumstances because I hadn't yet learned the lesson He wanted me to learn. But when my sincere prayer finally became, "Lord, teach me what You want me to learn in this," then that particular trial went away. I once heard Chuck Swindoll say that when we understand and accept the fact that life is difficult—then it ceases to be difficult.

Chuck Swindoll also tells how, in ancient times, clay pots were tempered with fire. If the pot came out of the fire uncracked, the potter stamped the word *dokimas* on the pot, to show it had passed through the fire without breaking. In putting the pot in the fire, the potter's desire was not to see how quickly it would break, but to temper it so it could withstand the thumps and bumps it would take during its life as a pot. Any pots that did crack in the fire were used for garbage, because they would leak if water, wine, olive oil or some other precious liquid were placed inside.

I think that's a picture of what we go through too. God does not put us in the fire to see how soon we will break. He wants to burn the impurities out of our life, so we might more closely resemble Christ. If the fire breaks us, then we are of no use to anyone, except to hold a little garbage.

Bible teacher Kay Arthur tells how the silversmith puts silver ore in the crucible and turns up the heat. After a while he takes out the ore to see if the impurities have burned off.

If the silver is still not pure, he puts it back in the fire and turns up the heat a little more. His goal is to take it out of the furnace and be able to see his reflection in the metal.

That's exactly what God wants to do with us. When He puts us through the fiery trials and struggles of life, we feel the heat, but as a result some of the impurities burn out of our life. God's goal, like the silversmith's, is that His reflection will be visible when He takes the ore (us) out of the furnace. That is my highest goal—to reflect the image of Christ to other people. I fall short, for sure, but it is a worthy goal.

Are you allowing God to process you into the image of Christ? Or are you fighting your circumstances, questioning God, or feeling like quitting or running away? I've felt that way at times, but I've always come again to the realization that God allows these things in my life for a purpose, and many times I can even see at least part of His purpose for the trial soon after it's over. It's natural to want to run away from problems; it's SUPERNATURAL to go through them, trusting God and patiently waiting for His view of them to become clear to us.

One of the ways to escape feeling blue and discouraged about your lot in life is to count your blessings. On my list of blessings I have good health, a wonderful wife, three wonderful kids, a wonderful daughter-in-law, a perfect granddaughter, a perfect puppy, a bunch of perfect cats, a good job, a successful business, and a host of other things. After you've made your own list of blessings, begin another list of all the ways God has answered your specific prayers. Think about each one, and ask yourself whether He could do something like it again. All of a sudden you won't be feeling so bad, and can once again put into effect Hebrews 12:12-13:

So take a new grip with your tired hands, stand firm on your shaky legs and mark out a straight, smooth path for your feet so that those who follow you though weak and lame will not fall and hurt themselves, but become strong.

This passage says to me that it's okay for me to feel tired and shaky, but even then there comes a time to get up again so the people watching me will be encouraged. If I can make it, they can too.

There's even a well-known document that should make us feel better when we fail. It's called the Declaration of Independence—the document that started our nation's life. We reverence it and are awed by its vision. But look at it closely and you'll find several errors—a word left out here, a misspelling there, etc. Of higher priority than making a perfect copy were the realities of the moment: This was already the 123rd version or so, the Continental Congress had a new nation to govern, the Redcoats were coming, it was hot that day, and besides July 4th is a holiday and who wants to recopy something on a holiday, right? I don't blame them for just getting on with their lives—just like we're to do when we make a mistake. Ask God's forgiveness, make restitution with anyone you have hurt or offended, put the past in the past, and get up once again to mark out the path God wants for your life.

The Bible says He has put our sins away from us "as far as the east is from the west." And the east and west never meet. The Bible also points out that God chooses not to remember our past sin. If we go to him to ask His forgiveness, it's as if He says, "This is the first time, isn't it?" We have to admit we've come to Him with the same problem before. We are in agony with a broken spirit. Remembering all those other times, we hate to have to ask His forgiveness again—but if God chooses not to remember our past sin, why in the world do we keep wallowing in it? Put a mark on the mirror you look into each morning, a mark that says, "The past has passed, today is a new day, and no longer will I remember what God has forgotten." Let's learn from our mistakes, but then go forward rather than being mired down by looking back.

There is a caution related to our view of God's grace

and forgiveness, however, and the apostle Paul touches on it in Romans 3:5-8.

"But," some say, "our breaking faith with God is good; our sins serve a good purpose, for people will notice how good God is when they see how bad we are. Is it fair, then, for him to punish us when our sins are helping him?" (That is the way some people talk.) God forbid! Then what kind of God would he be to overlook sin? How could he ever condemn anyone?...If you follow through with that idea you come to this: the worse we are, the better God likes it! But the damnation of those who say such things is just.

We've had a number of so-called Christian men leave their wives for other women. One of them even said that his actions were okay because God is a forgiving God. I can't read God's mind, nor has He asked me to be His counselor; but I believe that somehow, someway, this young man is going to miss God's blessings either here or in heaven, if in fact he is a Christian in the first place. A Christian, remember, cannot keep shaking his fist at God by living in habitual sin. If he continues to do this, he simply does not have Christ in him. He might know a lot about God and Christ, and could even believe Christ died on the cross to pay the sacrifice for our sins (demons know all this too). He has just never taken the step to truly accept and live by these facts personally. This type of person still wants to do things his own way, and of course that's the bottom line of sin—doing things our way instead of God's. It started with Adam and Eve, as you'll remember.

We've known personally a number of pastors who lost their ministries because of immorality. In every case except one, we see no broken spirit, no agonizing over their sin and over how they've hurt the people they have failed. We get the impression they are sorry they got CAUGHT, but that's about it. If people who fail would exhibit a broken and contrite heart over how they had failed God, rather than talking about how it was someone else's fault or about all the people who were out to get them, the Christian community would accept them back with open hearts and arms. We all know that we too could fall the same way they have. But if the person who falls is a pastor, then I think he's lost the privilege to serve in that position, because the requirements are very strict:

For a pastor must be a good man whose life cannot be spoken against. He must have only one wife, and he must be hard working and thoughtful, orderly, and full of good deeds. He must enjoy having guests in his home, and must be a good Bible teacher. He must not be a drinker or quarrelsome, but he must be gentle and kind, and not be one who loves money. (1 Timothy 3:2-3)

We all fail at times. We all must ask for forgiveness from God and from others we have hurt. But then let's allow God to bury our past failures, and then focus on the present and the future, and obey Him step by step as He makes us the kind of men and women He wants us to be.

(BARB:) We mentioned earlier how the woman reflects back to the man exactly what he has been giving her. I think it's interesting to note that a woman gets most of her self-esteem from her relationship with her husband, but a man usually gets his self-esteem from his work. Even if a woman works in the marketplace, most of her good feelings come when her home and family are in order.

While men tend to be a little more objective in their approach to life, women tend to relate everything to themselves. Suppose a woman's husband said something at dinner like, "Where did you get this meat?" The woman would probably reply, "What's wrong with it?" All the husband wanted to know is whether it was from Safeway or the small meat shop down the street. Usually he is impressed with how good it is, rather than how bad. The same thing would probably happen if the man looked at the woman on the way to church and said, "Where did you get that dress?" Again, her reply would probably be, "What's wrong with it?"

Even the fears of a man and women tend to be different, fears that are felt when we don't treat our mates as the Lord told us to. When a wife is not in her role of being submissive—respecting and loving her husband with friendship and admiration—her husband realizes his two greatest fears. The first is the fear of failure. The second is the fear of being dominated by a woman.

These are God-given fears. God made men to be providers and protectors and to be in headship. When we as women don't give our husbands the trust and respect that such a role deserves, they feel like failures. You know how it is: The first time our husbands make a mistake, we decide to take over. We tell them what they should or should not have done. They feel they have failed, and if they do as we say, they feel like they have been dominated by a woman.

When a husband does not live out his role of loving unconditionally and giving himself up for his wife, then she feels her greatest fear, which is the fear of being taken for granted. He wants her to cook his meals, take care of the kids, make sure he has clean clothes in his drawer, and keep his house clean. In addition, he expects her to go to all his business parties and meetings. But he never includes her in his thoughts or talks to her as a friend. He spends money for things that *he* wants, but tells his wife she is spending too much on food or clothes or whatever.

He makes decisions that involve her future as well as his, but never talks over those decisions with her. He teases her about how much she weighs and about getting older, and then wonders why she doesn't want to go to bed with him. She has been treated like a thing, rather than the lovely person she thought he saw in her before they were married. She has been taken for granted.

If we would obey what the Lord tells us to do as husbands and wives, we could avoid having to be defensive with one another all the time. The Lord says in Matthew 6, "Whatever you want others to do for you, do so for them." That's called the Golden Rule. Even our non-Christian friends have heard of that one. And it works.

I can surely relate to what Barb is saying about a man's fears. Personally, I think the fear of failure is much more a factor than the fear of being dominated by a woman. The second one might be instinctive, but the failure thing is right in front of our eyes all the time. I experience this when she suggests I have the wrong tie on, or missed some places while mowing the lawn, or cut the wrong limb on the tree I was pruning. All she is doing is giving her opinion. She is still examining and discussing the matter, but I assume a final judgment has been made against me, and I've failed again.

The key to handling this difference of opinions without producing fear is to simply accept each other's gifts and differences, and then compromise. For instance, we used to have conflicts in the airport. Each of us has our own "right" ideas on what to do when. One of us would want to get the luggage first, the other would want to get the rental car. One of us would want to go right to the gate, the other would want to stop for coffee (guess which one).

Then one time everything seemed to go quite smoothly. After we sat down in the waiting area at the gate, I commented on how well things had gone. Barb said in her most sarcastic voice, "That's because I did everything YOU wanted." Barb swears it was a nice voice, but it didn't sound very nice to me, so I got silent for a while. Anyway, since then she has delegated airports to me, just as I 've delegated navigation in the car to her.

Another area in which we had to work out a compromise was in getting a hotel room. I was the firstborn kid in my family, so I usually follow the rules. So if the person at the front desk says we are in Room 202, then I feel God decreed before the foundation of the world that we were to stay in 202. However, I married someone who without so much as a thought wants to look at Rooms 306 and 405, because 202 smelled bad, or the view is of the parking lot, or it has the wrong size bed. This used to irritate me no end, but after we agreed not to sweat the little things, I put a book in my coat pocket. Now when we go into a hotel room, I don't start to unpack or even take off my coat. I just grab my book, head for the nearest chair and wait to see if the room passes inspection. I realized she has as much right to change rooms as I do to follow the "rules." She usually does find a better room, but by nature I would never put anyone out looking around for it.

Or let's take the fact that Barb feels deadlines are "guidelines." Again, being a firstborn, I want to be on time when we go out. It took me a while to figure out what was going on when I would be out in the car ready to go to church or somewhere, and no Barb. I would wait and wait, then go back into the house to find her. Guess what she would be doing? Making the beds, cleaning the kitchen, or hanging up kids' clothes. What in the world does that have to do with going where we are supposed to be going? Well, she just doesn't want to come home to a mess, and after all, if we're a little late, so what? No one will care much. I agree now, but it took me a few years.

Or let's take the fact that Barb feels that restaurant menus are also guidelines. Restaurants spend thousands of dollars planning, printing and distributing menus, and Barb wants to change them. "Could you add a salad to that entrée please…with two different kinds of dressing, one on the side...and muffins instead of bread...and add a wedge of lemon please?" Can you believe Barb disrupting the forces of commerce like that?

> What's true on this for Chuck and me can be seen in many marriages: So often it's our different perspectives on the little things that can make the husband uncomfortable. Men tend to be more stable when it comes to the big things—handling earthquakes, disease, disasters, war—but can go out of their mind if their nail clippers are missing. Chuck has been known to go out and buy ten flashlights or five pairs of scissors or six sets of nail clippers, just because the one he usually uses is missing.
>
> While men tend to have their eyes set on the big goal down the road, and don't want to be bothered by disruptions in the little details, women often seem able to have a more in-depth concentration on the details of the moment—and can get more involved in the day-to-day finer points.

The bottom line is this: Compromise as much as you can on the little things like airport routines, hotel rooms, and restaurant orders. Go with the gifts each person has. One will be detailed, the other loose. One will be a good navigator, the other will get lost easily. One wants to follow the rules, one wants to bend them when it doesn't really matter. Allow each other to be different. Say "It's okay" rather than "It's wrong."

By the way, this not only is a valuable approach in marriage, but it also works great with your co-worker, your neighbor, the other members on the committee, and everyone else you deal with in life.

15

Pursuing Peace ...and Love

(CHUCK:) Someone has wisely said, "If you love something, let it go. If it's yours, it will come back to you; if it doesn't come back, it was never really yours in the first place." This principle of releasing comes into play in helping us solve marriage conflicts.

I had lunch with a young media friend the other day. Now, when I'm with men I always try to get the subject around to marriage, because most men don't get around to learning much about it. I asked him how everything was going at home, and he said things were great—except that his wife wanted to go on vacation to Phoenix in August. He had put his foot down. It would be way too hot, and besides, they couldn't afford it. He and his wife were having some heated discussions over this.

He asked my advice, so I suggested that since he was to die for his wife, he should make arrangements to go to Phoenix in August. I suggested he tell her that she was the most important thing in his life, and if she wanted to go to Phoenix in August he would be glad to go with her. I added, however, that he probably would not have to go. He didn't quite understand that, but decided to take my advice. He sent a note a few days later to report that they were not going to Phoenix in August. His wife thought it would be too hot, and they really couldn't afford it.

They had a power struggle going. He was insisting they would not go to Phoenix in August. She was resisting him and was determined that they WOULD go. When he released her, she did the right thing.

A couple once came to us for counsel on what to do with a rebellious teenager. She wasn't awful, but in her spirit she was constantly resisting the family. She was almost eighteen, so we suggested they release her—and let God put the pressure on her to be less resistant to the family. We suggested they tell her that because she was almost an adult, they would no longer tell her what to do; they were turning her over to God. They would be her support, however, if she needed them. The parents told her this, and it wasn't long before she was back in the family unit with a positive attitude.

Somehow parents think that if they give their advice or state their opinion just one more time (even though they've said the same thing 798 times before), this time the teenager will hear it. But often, all it does is drive the teenager further away. We also worry that if we release our older teenage children, they might go out and get pregnant, become an alcoholic, and start doing hard drugs—and they might. But they're already breaking the rules anyway, so maybe if you stop being their Holy Spirit and become their friend, ready to step in if needed, they will come back to what they know are your standards.

Our son Tim is a creative, right-brain person. As a child he had two problems. The first was that his parents didn't know anything about brain-wiring, and the second was that most schools focus on left-brain subjects like science, reading, arithmetic, biology, chemistry, and so on... Right-brain subjects like art and music are shuffled into the if-you-can't-do-anything-else category.

Tim was a dreamer like most creative people are. He would sit in class and suddenly wake up realizing the teacher had been talking for fifteen minutes and he hadn't the foggiest notion what she was saying. Of course, his grades reflected this.

He also seemed to be always a half step out of phase with the rest of the family. If we wanted to go to the zoo, he wanted to go to the beach. If we wanted to look at slides, he wanted to look at movies. If I wanted him to mow the lawn, he decided to clean out the garage. I only wish I had known then what made him tick. He was creative. Growing up he spent hours underneath his toy car "fixing" it. He took apart every mechanical item he could find—every clock, toaster, recorder and whatever—including some things I wished he hadn't taken apart. If only I had the maturity back then to care more about how Tim was put together than about the things he took apart.

He got into the wrong crowd because they accepted him for who he was. He loved to help people in trouble, and this helped cement their relationships. Through all this Tim was a fortress as far as not bending to peer pressure. He was never into drugs, alcohol, or sexual immorality. He was a wonderful kid—but just a little out of step with the family, and we didn't know why. He knocked over a gas pump one time with his car, and for discipline he was to go through the book of Proverbs and write out in longhand every verse that had the word "son" in it. Then he was to explain to me what the verses meant. He worked and worked and even took his Bible to school.

Finally one morning he woke me up and wanted to go over the Scriptures with me. We had gone over only a few verses before I noticed he had missed one of the key ones. I pointed this out and he said, "Even the ones that don't apply?" The one he missed was of course one of the zingers that REALLY applied. He went back to work and later we went over the verses, both of us in tears, as we realized just what God had in mind for a son.

As he approached eighteen years of age, we decided to release him to God, knowing He would put pressure on Tim if He wanted him to change some of his habits and lifestyle. We felt we had done all we could. Saying it one more time would not make any difference. So we told him he was now responsible directly to God, not to us. We would always be his parents. Our home would always be his home. We would help whenever he wanted. But he was free to have any companions he wanted, to come in anytime day or night, or to have any lifestyle he wanted. All of a sudden he was calling us at 3 a.m. and saying, "Don't worry, I'm just over here at Rob's." We weren't worrying, we were asleep. We knew God was watching out for him. Tim was now GOD'S responsibility, not ours. It wasn't long before Tim was coming home at midnight; then he started getting to bed by 10:30.

He escaped high school with a 1.9 grade point average, and looked at his diploma as a pardon. Since he could take the motor out of his car every afternoon, dust it off and make it run again, we decided to encourage him to go to a diesel mechanics school. He signed up and began to get straight A's. He hated math in school, but now he was bringing home fractions and decimal problems. I mentioned to him that his homework looked a lot like math. He said it wasn't math, it was piston ratios and valve clearances. Someone had finally hit his hot button, and we were so grateful. He is now a manager of a successful diesel shop in Seattle.

Let me say one more thing about kids. If I had it to do over again, I would not mention one thing about grades. For certain I would never punish for "bad" grades. I would hardly even mention them. I just don't think they mean that much, and they surely are not worth family battles with the resultant damage to a child's self-esteem.

I'm ancient, and truthfully I've never had one person—even prospective bosses—ask me whether I ever took algebra in school, and what grade I got. No one seems to have cared that I took geology and got a B. I had a D in history at midsemester before bringing it up to a B by the end of the term, but WHO CARES? The marketplace surely doesn't. All they want to know is whether you can do the job.

I think the author of *The One Minute Manager* has the right idea. He notes that when a kid brings home two C's and a D, most parents climb all over the D: "What are you doing, dreaming?" "Why don't you pay attention?" etc. He suggests saying something like, "Two C's...WOW! You really must be working!" Have a block party with a Blue Angels flyover. Put your son or daughter on a pedestal and point to them, saying, "There's my son—he got two C's!" Guess what will happen on the next report card? The D comes up to a C and one of the C's goes to a B. It felt so good they want more.

Parents are funny, getting all uptight about whether their kids will make it in life. Now as a grandparent I can view kids with a lot more patience than I ever viewed my own.

The other day I was feeding Kjersten, the world's most perfect grandchild. She had climbed up on a small bar we have between the kitchen and dining room. She would stand up, lay down, put her head between her knees, lay on her back, and stand on her head. Wherever her mouth was, I would put the food. But if she had been MY child, I would have had her sit up straight, and clean up her plate, and not squirm, and both of us would have had a miserable time.

I took her to a lake in Seattle. She was only two at the time, and really didn't know what a lake was all about. She would run toward the water's edge and just before she fell in I would gently grab her collar and stop her forward motion. Now if she had been MY child, I would have chained her to a tree fifteen feet away from the water and put three life-jackets on her.

We had a peanut party the other day. In attendance were me, Kjersten, Muffit our dog, and the spotted cat. The four of us sat around on the kitchen floor. I would shell a peanut for Kjersten, then shell one for Muffit, then one for the cat, then one for me, and then back to Kjersten. Sure we made a mess on the floor, but it was easy to clean up.

We went to the state fair recently. We had those awesome greasy hamburgers with onions. So what if Kjersten put too much ketchup on her fries, or ate the mayonnaise straight out of the little plastic bag, or swallowed the sugarless gum, or got chocolate on her pants? WHO CARES? I'm afraid parents do, so Kjersten's mom Tammie and I have worked out a deal: Tammie is to pull her earlobe if I am letting Kjersten do something that's against her parents' rules.

This is another reason I'm putting off my heart attack as long as I can. I just don't think anyone else would know how to be a Grandpa to Kjersten. We have a routine when she comes to visit. (By the way, I always ask Tammie to bring three or four different sets of clothes because we might get some of them dirty or wet.) First of all she jumps in my arms and says, "Pay sand," so we go to the sand box for a while and cook broccoli and fix tea. Then we have to swing for awhile. Then we have to "drive" for a while, and by coincidence there is some gum in the glove compartment. And since I have never read one Scripture verse that says you can chew only one stick at a time, we have a whole pack at once. Then we ride our trike for a while. Then we go in the house and play "tents." This is where we put blankets over some chairs in the front room. Then we have to go downstairs where the sound-activated fish is mounted on the wall. We clap our hands to make it move. Then she gets the change out of my pocket to put in the gumball machine in my office. Then we wash the dishes. I get some clean ones out of the cupboard and steady her as she stands on a stool "washing" things. It is hard for her to remember not to squirt the spray toward the windows, but what's a little water? Windows don't rust. Then, since she is pretty well soaked after doing the dishes, we take a bath in the sink. Then we dry off and read some books. Now don't you think that is too complicated for just anyone to do?

And by the way, I don't agree with those family critics who suggest I am spoiling her. I remember so clearly there were things I could do at MY grandparents' home that I wouldn't expect to do at my parents' home. I don't remember being traumatized. I think I just accepted the difference and didn't worry too much about trying to get away with something at home.

It just occurred to me what an amazing coincidence it is to have the World's Most Perfect Grandchildren, the World's Most Perfect Puppy and the World's Most Perfect Cat all in the same family. That's one for the Guinness Book of Records, don't you think?

Why can't we relax with our kids a little more? Maybe that's why God invented grandparents. They have more time to watch the worms.

I want to repeat a very important fact for parents: The root word for discipline is the same one as for disciple. When someone asks us to disciple them, we are patient, kind, loving, and never get angry or loud. We think the best of that person, and are usually willing to give him lots of second chances. Why don't we do the same thing with our kids as we "disciple" them? It's the same word, same principle—just different people.

We need to release our wives and husbands too. We've worked with numerous people whose mates had run off with someone else or were having an affair, or were just resistant to continuing the relationship. One couple in particular comes to mind. The man came into my life at a lunch meeting. He was miserable. His wife had left him and was dating someone else. He was trying very hard to get her back, but was smothering her with his requests. First we suggested that he needed supernatural power to get through this problem, and we introduced him to Jesus Christ. He became a Christian and began giving his wife to the Lord and not trying so hard to get her back on his own. He focused on being the man HE should be, rather than on what she was doing wrong. She saw this change in him, and was open to coming to a party in our home. She noticed we didn't have our hair in a bun, walk around with our hands folded all the time, or wear big wooden crosses or a flat hat like religious folks on TV do. We looked and acted almost "normal." It wasn't long before she responded to this new spirit she was feeling from her husband, and they came up hand-in-hand one day and announced they had gotten back together. Later the wife became a Christian too. They still have conflicts to this day—so do Barb and I. But now they have the Lord to give them insights into how to work out a marriage relationship.

It's usually the other way around: The husband is out wandering, and the wife is left emotionally destitute. Again, the first thing she has to do is get supernatural help by asking Jesus Christ into her life. Then she has to release her husband and let God put the pressure on him to return. After all, God is as concerned about your marriage as you are—more so, I'm sure. Instead of crying and begging and acting weak, you become strong because Christ's strength is now in you. You picture your husband as handicapped. Picture him as not being able to control himself. He just doesn't have the supernatural ability to do the right thing. In your prayers, ask God to bring along someone your husband can respect who can help him find God's help. Your role, however, is just an observer. The Bible says if the non-Christian husband or wife wants to leave, let them. But usually what happens is they are so taken by your quiet and gentle spirit, they are attracted back to you. Sometimes they do leave. It surely is not automatic or one-hundred-percent certain that they will stay, but it is unusual if they are not attracted by the new you.

This doesn't mean a wife or husband becomes a doormat or ceases to give personal opinions. It just means that if you feel you've tried everything you know to get their attention or help them change, turn them over to God. He puts better pressure on them than we do.

If your husband never picks up his socks, if your wife never shines the silverware, if he never becomes interested in spiritual things, if she never keeps the flower beds weeded ...so what? Release—accept—serve—minister to your wife or husband, without trying to change them.

(BARB:) The reason we can let our mates be who they are, rather than who we want them to be, is that we're experiencing the fruit of the Spirit called meekness—which is strength under control. We are under the control of the Holy Spirit within us. I've already told you that meekness is a serenity of spirit, accepting everything that comes into our lives as coming from the hand of God, whether we think it is good or bad. The reason we can look at trials this way is because we know God rules over all. He is in control of every situation that comes into our lives. He could have prevented the situation if He had wanted to. He allows circumstances in our lives to mold us and make us into His image. Trials comes to us, to mature us, to make us complete and lacking in nothing. God never tempts us, yet He does design trials for us once in a while. These trials aren't designed by Him to trip us up, but to prove our faith:

In this you greatly rejoice, even though now for a little while, if necessary, you have been distressed by various trials, that the proof of your faith, being more precious than gold which is perishable, even though tested by fire, may be found to result in praise and glory and honor at the revelation of Jesus Christ. (1 Peter 1:6-7)

After thirty-three years of marriage I'm amazed sometimes at how different Chuck and I still are, and how so many of these differences have led to disagreements and conflicts. My dream for marriage was to never have arguments, and to live in peace with each other all the time, and Chuck's dream for marriage was the same. But after we got married we discovered the hard way how we even disagreed on how to handle disagreements, as we've mentioned earlier. Jesus' words in Matthew 5:9 have been helpful in understanding more about this:

Blessed are the peacemakers, for they shall be called the sons of God.

He didn't say peaceKEEPERS, but peaceMAKERS. On the surface, the peacekeeper appears calm. But inside there can be a boiling cauldron of unspoken thoughts which can turn into a root of bitterness. We are told in Hebrews 12:14-15,

Pursue after peace with all men, and the sanctification (which means "being set apart for God's use only") *without which no one will see the Lord. See to it that no one comes short of the grace of God; that no root of bitterness springing up causes trouble, and by it many be defiled.*

To be a peacemaker, one must "pursue after peace." The problem is, when someone pursues peace, he or she often stirs up trouble trying to reach a peaceful conclusion. By the way, when a wife gives her opinion or feelings to her husband, his reaction may be so harsh that she becomes afraid. After she experiences this a few times, she may quit giving her true opinions.

There have been times in our relationship where I have not been completely honest with Chuck because I just couldn't bear his disapproval again. It's not easy to always have a different opinion than your husband. Most wives don't plan to disagree on purpose with their husbands—it's just that we do think about things differently than they do.

The usual pattern, when Chuck and I had a disagreement, would be for him to withdraw. I would often ask him, "Can we talk?" He took this as a sign of trouble. To me, it meant I was trying to make peace. We didn't know it at the time, but I was being a peacemaker, and Chuck was being a peacekeeper.

As we've said before, the nonexpressive finds peacekeeping much more comfortable than communication about the disagreement. On the other hand, the expressive finds it much easier to pursue communication, and perceives that this is vital for the relationship. Maybe this is why the Lord puts these two different types together so often. He knows that bitterness might result if two nonexpressives were married to each other.

When a person is meek, and knows that whatever comes into their lives is ordained by God, then they can live through the harsh replies or the disapproval, and be a peacemaker. Sometimes peacemakers have to go through a lot of guff before peace is made. Often they are attacked personally. Peacemakers may even be accused of disrupting the peace. It's not easy to be a peacemaker, but it is the best way, because that's what the Lord commands.

Our friends Norm and Bobbe Evans gave Barb and I a tape by Gary Chapman talking about the various types of love languages. We think this is one of the most important ideas any couple could have, so we'll give you a quick overview.

But we recommend you get the complete picture from Dr. Chapman's material.

He suggests that there are five basic love languages: touch, talking (or communication), serving, giving gifts, and encouraging words. The problem is that we tend to talk to others in our own language. A person with touch as a love language is usually a huggy person. They might reach out and touch you on the arm to make a point. They may pat you on the back or reach over and take your hand for a minute.

A person with talking as his love language wants deep, intimate sharing of his life with another person. This also includes spending time with each other—quality time. A person who serves is one who likes to do things for people. He or she will help clean up the kitchen, pick up the chairs at church, mow the neighbor's lawn when they go on vacation, or bring you a hot cup of coffee.

Sometimes people also show love by giving gifts, and sometimes their love is shown by offering encouraging words—"You did a great job today," "You're the best employee we have," "That solo was one of the finest I've heard," "I love the way you drive so carefully."

Dr. Chapman tells of a couple that came to him for counseling. The wife was saying, "My husband just doesn't love me anymore." The husband said, "What do you mean? I wash the dishes while you're at work, take care of the kids when they come from school, mow the lawn, do the laundry and keep the house clean." She said, "But you don't TALK to me." He said, "Yes I do. I say, 'Hello,' 'How was work?' 'What do you want to watch on TV?' "

What's happening here, of course, is that he was talking to her in his own love language—serving. She is not feeling loved because her love language was talking and communication. Some husbands are amazed that their wives don't feel loved after being given diamonds, big houses, nice cars, fur coats—everything materially they could possible want.

His language might be giving gifts, but the wife's language might be touch or talking. The idea is to find out what your mate's love language is and talk to them in that language rather than in your own.

Bobbe tells of the time her kitchen radio broke. Norm's primary language is touch, but he stopped by a store and bought a small little radio that he felt didn't amount to much but was all he could find, and gave it to Bobbe. She went out of her mind; she felt so loved. Her love language is gifts. To him it was just a cheap little radio. To her it proved his love because he gave her something.

Take a moment right now and try to determine what your mate's love language is. Usually a person will have one special way—one "language"—in which they best understand love. Unfortunately, Barb understands all five, which really keeps me hopping.

16

Hupotasso
Whoopee!

(CHUCK:) I suppose no book on marriage is complete without some discussion of sex. After all, that's the icing, yet there is still so much misunderstanding and uncomfortableness in the Christian community about discussing it. I suppose the world has so contaminated this aspect of marriage that we've gotten the mistaken idea there's something inherently wrong with it. I suppose it also could stem from Victorian holdovers.

If a person spends any time at all in the Bible, they just have to come to the conclusion that sex was God's idea. He stayed up late three nights in a row inventing it. He is the One who has blessed it and sanctified it, and wants people to enjoy it inside the marriage relationship—and that's where the world gets messed up. Remember when President Reagan was ridiculed in the press for suggesting that the best way to prevent AIDS was to not have sexual relationships outside marriage? He was treated like a fool, and yet that suggestion is EXACTLY what would have prevented AIDS and most every other venereal disease down through history. AIDS is not some judgment God made up for this generation. I believe He set the plan in motion from the beginning of time. He knew the world would corrupt the sexual process, so He set up some natural consequences to help them remember to do it His way. It's similar to the natural law of gravity. If we jump off a cliff, we can be the most spiritual person on the face of the earth and still fall to the rocks below. If we violate God's natural law of marriage, then we'll suffer the consequences for our disobedience. It's as simple as that.

One of the most fascinating books I've read recently is George Gilder's *Men and Marriage*. I recommend it highly. Part of what he stresses is the tragedy of young women giving up their prime childbearing years for a career and a things-oriented lifestyle, when they would have plenty of time after the children are gone for their career and accumulation of things. The problem is that, when the woman gets around to marriage at age thirty-five or so, there is only a five percent chance she will find someone.

Gilder talks about how many young women are attracted to older men with money and power—but these men are usually married. A man like that will often lead along a young woman into an affair for a few years, and then he dumps her after he's had his fun and decides to go back home to his wife and children. She ends up wasting her prime childbearing years with someone who seldom will give her what she wants—security and a commitment.

Because women are more sexually liberated these days, more and more single men feel inadequate, especially when a woman is making more money than he is. This, Gilder suggests, is one of the prime causes of homosexuality. Some men feel inadequate and abased, so they act abased. He feels the breakdown of the monogamous marriage relationship is causing most of the ills in today's society, and I couldn't agree with him more. We see his observations verified in the headlines daily.

Therefore, as we make our comments, you can assume we feel that all sexual activity should be within the bounds of marriage. After all, it takes more creativity to keep one woman satisfied for fifty years, than multiple women during a series of one-night stands. And it's a lot more satisfying to have the same partner for life, despite what the world may say.

We men had a big shock a few years ago when Ann Landers reported that seventy-two percent of the women surveyed would rather have a hug than go to bed with their husbands. Personally, I think the figure is low. There is a bright side, however, because this means that twenty-eight percent of you women reading this book attack your husband in his workshop. And you don't have to tell me who you are—I can tell by the smile on your husband's face.

Do you realize that for the normal man, having sex with his wife is the funnest thing he does? It beats tennis, his workshop, even Monday Night Football. You women may not believe me when I say it's that much pleasure to him; but just trust me. You also probably think that sex is all a man thinks about. Well, you're right, especially if you haven't taken him to bed for three weeks. He can get turned on by a cartoon in the newspaper, let alone by the magazine covers he's exposed to as he goes about his daily business. You see, men have a pressure system, and when the gage gets into the red you need to do something about that.

As usual, the Bible has the answer. In 1 Corinthians 7 couples are instructed to come together regularly so Satan cannot tempt us to stray outside of marriage. I looked up the word "regularly" in the Greek. It is *hupotasso WHOOPEE*, which means three or more times a week. Don't blame me, ladies—look up the Greek for yourself. Barb says I could never keep up the pace. I say she has never tried me

The best way to keep your husband from running away with secretaries and next-door neighbors is to keep him happy at home, especially sexually. If all a man has to look forward to when he comes home is the greeting "You're late" from a person who looks like she just got off the boat, why would he want to come home? Sure you have your nightgown on sometimes, but it has feet in it.

Just once before he dies—just once—send the kids to the neighbors, cook his favorite meal, add a little candlelight, maybe meet him at the door with nothing on but a little apron (be careful you don't surprise the milkman), look and smell like you did on your first date, then let nature take its course; delight in each other just as God intended. You only have to do this once, ladies, but this is an evening he will remember for the rest of his life.

Men, too, need more understanding of what a woman needs sexually. He is like a light switch: On/Off. She is like an iron: slowly heating up...slowly cooling down. Sometimes before she gets her mind off what they had for dinner the man has switched on and off and is snoring—"Who was that masked man anyway?" Most men are so selfish and so ignorant, and don't spend much time learning how their wife is designed. If a man never touches his wife unless he wants to go to bed, she feels used. Gary Smalley suggests that a woman needs twelve nonsexual touches a day just to keep her sanity. This means holding her hand in the car, putting your arm around her in church or at the movies, reaching over at dinner and touching her arm.

Men like to be spontaneous. Many women do not. Barb likes to have us plan in advance when we'll be getting together. It IS nicer when you can anticipate it, even though sometimes I think a woman could just do a man a favor in the porch swing or in front of the fireplace once in a while without a great deal of advance notice. Again, it's just one of the differences we experience. Women are turned on by a relationship—touching, communicating, caring, being sensitive, remembering birthdays and holidays, taking walks, doing little extra things around the house with no expectation of return.

There have been studies indicating that a man thinks about sex once every thirty seconds, which is unbelievable. I know that's an exaggeration, because I've gone a minute and a half before.

We're often asked during our seminars whether there's sex after age fifty. What a ridiculous question. Of COURSE there is—and the one in the spring is especially nice.

17

Grounds for a Great Marriage

(CHUCK:) Again, the only reason Barb and I can possibly be of help to you in your marriage relationship is that God has allowed us to go through struggles and problems. The key is going THROUGH the difficulties. Had we tried to get out of them, we would not be of any value to anyone. It's easy to walk away. It's tough to stay and work it out, but the feelings and satisfaction that come later are well worth the effort. As Scripture points out,

These trials are only to test your faith to see whether or not it is strong and pure. It is being tested as fire tests gold and purifies it—and your faith is far more precious to God than mere gold; so if your faith remains strong after being tried in the test tube of fiery trials, it will bring you much praise and glory and honor on the day of his return. (1 Peter 1:7)

God has never promised us protection from trials. I'm dismayed at the people teaching that God wants us healthy or rich or successful or prosperous. That's a lie of Satan. God has only promised us that He will be WITH US as we go through the fiery trials of life. He doesn't protect us from suffering—He protects us from our enemy Satan. Even though we don't always like the process, hurt is often the PROOF of obedience. The key to handling conflict is to have God's perspective. We need to look above, beyond and through the problem, allowing it to make us stronger rather than bitter. When I come to a barrier, I want relief, God wants maturity. Our commitment to Christ depends on our focus, not our circumstances.

Remember, the key to handling marriage conflict in the first place is a lifetime commitment. You need to verbally say to each other—actually repeating your marriage vows—that no matter what happens you will not leave the other person or seek a divorce. You WILL work things out even though there may be times when you feel like walking away. If you don't have this type of commitment, then one person in the relationship can emotionally blackmail the other by saying, "If you ever say that again I'm out of here." The one being blackmailed can never give his or her real feelings for fear the other will walk away. But when you have the foundation of "till death do us part," you can re-solve conflict in a healthy way.

Perhaps you have been divorced. You've already lived through what we are talking about. Don't be discouraged. Don't look back at the "what if's." Just make sure you've made this commitment to your present mate so you don't make the same mistake again.

We can't say this too often, but it takes SUPERNATU-RAL strength to make a marriage work. And the only source of that strength is having a personal relationship with Jesus Christ. I realize that to some of you it does not seem reasonable for a loving God to require such a narrow way for gaining entrance into heaven. So, to be fair, let's assume for a minute that the Christ we preach and teach is

NOT God. He was a fake, the eternal life He promised us is only wishful thinking, and we go back to dust when we die. For me, that's okay. I had a wonderful life here that was much more fulfilling and useful because of what I believed. I would not have traded one minute of it for anything I had observed in this world. On the other hand, if the Christ we preach really IS God and there is a real hell and a real judgment, then lots of people are in big trouble—eternally. This is not an easy message to hear. God is not some big Santa Claus sitting on His cloud who will change His mind at the last minute and let everyone into the pearly gates regardless of credentials.

When I go into the Kingdome to help with the Mariner chapels I have to show a pass to prove I belong there. If I don't have a pass, I don't get in. When people face the gates of heaven and God is there checking credentials, He's going to look at Christ's stamp on that life. It's not what we DO that saves us; it's WHO WE KNOW. If Christ has not stamped on that person the credentials ACCEPTED BY MY SACRIFICE, then even if he's the best church-goer in the world, and has worked with the poor for fifty-two years, gone on missions, taken a vow of silence, read through the Bible sixty-four times, never taken a drink of alcohol or lusted after a woman or cheated on his income tax—he still will not be able get through the gate. What a sad day that's going to be...but it doesn't have to be.

There's still time to check out the message of Christ and join His people in that eternity of blessing God has planned for us. I urge you to find a Bible now and ask God to show you the truth as you look up and think deeply about these verses: Romans 3:23 and 6:23; John 1:12, 3:16-17, and 5:24; and Ephesians 2:1-10. If you're convinced you need the sacrifice of Jesus Christ on the cross to take away your separation from God, and you want the living, resurrected Christ to take control of your life, I appeal to you to tell those things to God in prayer immediately—communicating also your true sorrow for your sins, and true joy and thankfulness for God's gift to the world of His Son Jesus.

Knowing and receiving this gift of God's love that cost Him so much is the true grounds for a successful marriage. Because God is real, and because this gift of His Son is real, and because the Bible is His Word and my authority, I will obey when it tells me to be a servant to Barb, to nourish and cherish her, to minister to her needs, to honor her as a "10," and to try to be everything she needs in a husband.

We have an awesome responsibility as Christian couples. The world is looking at us to see if we are at all different than they are. Can we handle our anger better? How do we endure suffering and hardships? Do we have more peace, security, joy, patience, kindness, tenderness, and forgiveness than the average person? Does our relationship with Christ seem to make any difference in our marriage? How do we handle our conflicts and setbacks or, for that matter, our successes? If we seem to have God's power in some of these areas, then our non-Christian friends will be open to our message sooner or later. But if they see no difference in our lives, then they surely don't need what we have.

It takes our own hard work—in the power of God's strength—to keep a marriage together, but it's worth far, far more than the effort.

> (BARB:) Chuck and I know there are times we fail to be all God wants us to be to Him and to each other. Yet the word that keeps coming back over and over to my mind is *obedience*. The way we have described to you may seem narrow, but the way of the Lord IS narrow. It's our own ways that are broad. The Lord said that just a few would be willing to walk on the narrow way, while many would choose the broad way.
>
> Chapter two of Paul's letter to the Romans describes how the religious people of his day were teaching others not to break the Law, while they themselves

were breaking it. They did some of the right things, but in their hearts they were going their own way. The Greek meaning for the word translated "breaking" refers to something which is not on the true line, either by falling short or going beyond it. Because we haven't known what the true line is—because we haven't put all the principles together in our minds—we have not walked on the true line. We may have been close, but still our relationships have not worked out right, because we haven't been on the narrow way.

Besides, some of the things the Lord tells us to do just don't seem right. They don't seem to make sense in "our circumstances." So we settle for short-term joy, but get long-term misery because we have not been willing to be obedient. We want happiness for ourselves RIGHT NOW. We just don't see the big picture—we don't see reality.

Chuck and I have quoted 1 Peter 5:7 several times already, but it fits here too. God invites us to cast all our anxiety on Him because He cares for us. He tells us to humble ourselves before Him so He can exalt us. If we choose to obey what He says, we may have short-term pain, but we will have long-term joy. Doing things His way always turns out right.

I believe the big picture must include knowing the final result of disobedience. Look again in Romans 2:

...but to those who are selfishly ambitious and do not obey the truth, but obey unrighteousness, wrath and indignation. There will be tribulation and distress for every soul of man who does evil, of the Jew first and also of the Greek, but glory and honor and peace to every man who does good, to the Jew first and also to the the Greek. For there is no partiality with God.

It's interesting to note that the meaning for the Greek words translated here as "tribulation" and "distress" includes "a pressing together, oppression, pressure, affliction, and straits." It is "anguish," "narrowness of place," and "constraint."

When we think about the mansions the Lord is preparing for those who obey Him, or the green pastures where He restores our souls, as mentioned in Psalm 23, we think of a broad way. In *this* life, however, if we stay on the broad way and do our own thing, we end up in a narrow and constricted place in the end. Our disobedience puts us in prison. On the other hand, if we stay on the narrow way in this life, we end up in a broad, spacious place. Our obedience gives us a freedom.

In the book of James we are told that the Word of God is the perfect law of liberty. Some people think if we do things the Lord's way, we will be put into prison, but the exact opposite is true. We're released from our confinements, and experience true freedom.

Our good works do not get us into heaven. What makes us Christian is trusting in the risen Lord Jesus Christ—acknowledging His death for our own sins, asking for forgiveness of our sins in His name (and receiving and believing in that forgiveness), and then following Him and accepting His authority over our lives. After trusting in Him, obeying Him keeps us on the narrow way. God asks us to enter through a small door onto the narrow path. When we do that, we experience the peace that comes from doing what the Lord says is right. We *stay* on the narrow way...a staying that equals obedience.

OUR WISH AND PRAYER for all who read this
book is that you will be obedient to God's
ways so you can experience not only eternal
life, but also a wonderful marriage.
You can have fun again with your mate, just
as you did when you were dating. You will
know a love for one another that you never
thought possible.

Obedience—that's the key.
And with the Lord's help you'll discover
that INCOMPATIBILITY can be grounds
for a GREAT marriage!

With God's Love and Blessings,

CHUCK & BARB

Bibliography

Books that offer encouragement and help
for your marriage:

Aldrich, Joseph C.
    LIFE-STYLE EVANGELISM.
    Portland, Ore.: Multnomah, 1981.

Arthur, Kay
    PRECEPT UPON PRECEPT
    Bible Study Series.
    Chattanooga: Reachout.

    HOW CAN I BE BLESSED.
    Old Tappan, N.J.: Power Books. (Revell)

    HOW CAN I LIVE.
    Power Books.

    LORD I WANT TO KNOW YOU.
    Power Books.

    TEACH ME HOW TO LIVE.
    Power Books.

Augsburger, David and John Faul.
    BEYOND ASSERTIVENESS.
    Waco, Tex.: Word, 1980.

Augsburger, David.
       CARING ENOUGH TO CONFRONT.
       Revised edition.
       Ventura, Calif.: Regal, 1980.

Barbeau, Clayton C.
       DELIVERING THE MALE.
       Minneapolis: Winston Press, 1982.

Bliss, Edwin C.
       GETTING THINGS DONE.
       New York: Charles Scribner's Sons, 1976.

Bramson, Robert N., M.D.
       COPING WITH DIFFICULT PEOPLE.
       Garden City, NY: Anchor Press, 1981.

Broadus, Loren.
       HOW TO STOP PROCRASTINATING & START
       LIVING.
       Minneapolis: Augsberg Publishing House, 1983.

Burkett, Larry.
       YOUR FINANCES IN CHANGING TIMES.
       Campus Crusade for Christ, Inc., 1975.

Carlson, Dwight L.
       HOW TO WIN OVER FATIGUE.
       Old Tappan, N.J.: Revell, 1974.

       OVERCOMING HURTS & ANGER.
       Eugene, Ore.: Harvest House, 1981.

Chapain, Marie.
       FREE TO BE THIN.
       Minneapolis: Bethany Fellowship, 1979.

Collins, Gary R.
        CHRISTIAN COUNSELING: A Comprehensive
        Guide.
        Waco, Tex.: Word, 1980.

Collins, Gary R., Ph.D.
        YOU CAN PROFIT FROM STRESS.
        Santa Ana, Calif: Vision House, 1977.

Colson, Charles W.
        BORN AGAIN.
        Old Tappan, N.J.: Revell, 1977.

Compolo, Tony.
        THE POWER DELUSION.
        Wheaton, Ill.: Victor.

Cook, Jerry, and Stanley C. Baldwin.
        LOVE, ACCEPTANCE & FORGIVENESS.
        Ventura, Calif.: Regal Books, 1979.

Crabb, Lawrence J., Jr.
        THE MARRIAGE BUILDER.
        Grand Rapids: Zondervan, 1982.

Dobson, James C.
        HIDE OR SEEK.
        Old Tappan, N.J.: Revell, 1974.

        LOVE MUST BE TOUGH.
        Waco, Tex.: Word, Inc., 1983.

        STRAIGHT TALK TO MEN AND THEIR WIVES.
        Waco, Tex.: Word, 1980.

        WHAT WIVES WISH THEIR HUSBANDS KNEW
        ABOUT WOMEN.
        Wheaton, Ill.: Tyndale House, 1975.

Douglass, Stephen.
MANAGING YOURSELF.
San Bernardino, Calif.: Here's Life, 1978.

Eliot, Dr. Robert S., and Dennis L. Breo.
IS IT WORTH DYING FOR?
New York: Bantam Books, 1984.

Engstrom, Ted W., and R. Alec MacKenzie.
MANAGING YOUR TIME.
Grand Rapids: Zondervan, 1967.

Fairfield, James G.T.
WHEN YOU DON'T AGREE.
Scottdale, PA: Herald Press, 1977.

Gilder, George.
MEN AND MARRIAGE.
Gretna, La.: Pelican, 1986.

Haggai, John Edmund.
HOW TO WIN OVER WORRY.
Grand Rapids: Zondervan, 1959.

Hansel, Tim.
WHEN I RELAX I FEEL GUILTY.
Elgin, Ill.: David C. Cook, 1979.

Hardisty, Margaret.
FOREVER MY LOVE.
Irvine, Calif.: Harvest House, 1975.

Hart, Archibald D.
ADRENALIN & STRESS.
Waco, Tex: Word, 1986.

DEPRESSION: COPING AND CARING.
Arcadia, Calif.: Cope Publications, 1981.

FEELING FREE.
Old Tappan, N.J.: Revell, 1979.

Hendricks, Howard G., and Ted Miller.
SAY IT WITH LOVE.
Wheaton, Ill.: SP Publications, 1972.

Hocking, David and Carole.
GOOD MARRIAGES TAKE TIME.
Eugene, Ore.: Harvest House, 1984.

Howard, J. Grant.
THE TRAUMA OF TRANSPARENCY.
Portland, Ore.: Multnomah, 1978.

Kehl, D.G.
CONTROL YOURSELF.
Grand Rapids: Zondervan, 1982.

Keller, W. Phillip.
TAMING TENSION.
Vantage Press, 1979.

LaHaye, Tim.
HOW TO WIN OVER DEPRESSION.
Grand Rapids: Zondervan, 1974.

SPIRIT-CONTROLLED TEMPERAMENT.
LaMesa, Calif.: Post, Inc., 1966.

TRANSFORMED TEMPERAMENTS.
Wheaton, Ill.: Tyndale, 1971.

UNDERSTANDING THE MALE TEMPERAMENT.
Old Tappan, N.J.: Revell, 1977.

Leman, Dr. Kevin.
THE BIRTH ORDER BOOK.
Old Tappan, N.J.: Revell, 1984.

Lewis, Margie M.
THE HURTING PARENT.
Grand Rapids: Zondervan, 1980.

Littauer, Florence.
LIVES ON THE MEND.
Waco, Tex.: Word, 1985.

Little, Paul E.
HOW TO GIVE AWAY YOUR FAITH.
Downers Grove, Ill.: Inter-Varsity Press, 1966.

Love, Sydney F.
MASTERY AND MANAGEMENT OF TIME.
Englewood Cliffs, N.J.: Prentice-Hall, 1978.

Mallory, James D., Jr. and Stanley C. Baldwin.
THE KINK & I: A Psychiatrist's Guide to Untwisted Living.
Wheaton, Ill.: Victor, 1973

Miller, Keith.
HABITATION OF DRAGONS.
Waco, Tex.: Word, 1970.

THE BECOMERS.
Waco, Tex.: Word, 1973.

Miller, Keith.
THE TASTE OF NEW WINE.
Waco, Tex.: Word, 1965.

Miller, Keith and Bruce Larson.
LIVING THE ADVENTURE: Faith & Hidden Difficulties.
Waco, Tex.: Word, 1975.

THE EDGE OF ADVENTURE.
Waco, Tex.: Word, 1974.

Minirth, Frank, M.D., Don Hawkins, Th. M., Paul Meier,
    M.D., and Richard Flournoy, Ph. D.
    HOW TO BEAT BURNOUT.
    Chicago: Moody Press, 1986.

Missildine, W. Hugh., MD.
    YOUR INNER CHILD OF THE PAST.
    New York: Simon & Schuster, 1963.

Montgomery, Robert L.
    LISTENING MADE EASY.
    New York: Amacom, 1981.

Morris, Henry M., ILL.
    EXPLORE THE WORD!.
    San Diego: Creation-Life, 1978.

Naifeh, Steven and Gregory White Smith.
    WHY CAN'T MEN OPEN UP?
    New York: Warner Books, 1984.

Nair, Ken.
    DISCOVERING THE MIND OF A WOMAN.
    Chicago: Chas. P. Young, 1982.

Narramore, Bruce.
    HELP! I'M A PARENT.
    Grand Rapids: Zondervan, 1972.

    WHY CHILDREN MISBEHAVE.
    Grand Rapids: Zondervan, 1980.

    YOU'RE SOMEONE SPECIAL.
    Grand Rapids: Zondervan, 1978.

    THE PSYCHOLOGY OF COUNSELING.
    Grand Rapids: Zondervan, 1972.

Ogilvie, Lloyd J.
   MAKING STRESS WORK FOR YOU.
   Waco, Tex.: Word Books Publisher, 1984.

Osborne, Cecil.
   RELEASE FROM FEAR AND ANXIETY.
   Waco, Tex.: Word Books Publisher, 1976.

   THE ART OF UNDERSTANDING YOUR MATE.
   Grand Rapids: Zondervan, 1970.

   THE ART OF UNDERSTANDING YOURSELF.
   Grand Rapids: Zondervan, 1967.

Petersen, J. Allen, editor.
   THE MARRIAGE AFFAIR.
   Wheaton, Ill.: Tyndale, 1971.

Ridenour, Fritz.
   HOW TO BE A CHRISTIAN WITHOUT BEING RE-
   LIGIOUS.
   Paraphrase—The Book of Romans.
   Glendale, Calif.: G/LPublications, 1967.

   WHAT TEENAGERS WISH THEIR PARENTS
   KNEW ABOUT KIDS.
   Waco, Tex.: Word, 1982

Rohrer, Norman and S. Philip Sutherland.
   FACING ANGER.
   Minneapolis: Augsburg Publishing House, 1981

   WHY AM I SHY?
   Minneapolis: Augsburg, 1978.

Schmidt, Paul F.
   COPING WITH DIFFICULT PEOPLE.
   Philadelphia: Westminster Press, 1980.

Shedd, Charlie and Martha.
CELEBRATION IN THE BEDROOM.
Waco, Tex.: Word Books Publisher, 1979.

Skoglund, Elizabeth R.
TO ANGER WITH LOVE.
New York: Harper & Row, 1977.

Smalley, Gary and Steve Scott.
FOR BETTER OR FOR BEST.
King of Prussia, Penn.: RM Marketing, 1979.

IF ONLY HE KNEW.
King of Prussia, Penn.: RM Marketing, 1979.

Smith, David W.
THE FRIENDLESS AMERICAN MALE.
Ventura, Calif.: Regal Books, 1978.

Stanley, Charles.
HOW TO KEEP YOUR KIDS ON YOUR TEAM.
Nashville: Oliver-Nelson Books, 1986.

Swindoll, Chuck.
IMPROVING YOUR SERVE: The Art of Unselfish Living.
Waco, Tex.: Word, 1981

Talley, Jim.
RECONCILABLE DIFFERENCES.
Nashville: Thomas Nelson, 1985.

Talley, Jim A. and Bobbie Reed.
TOO CLOSE TOO SOON.
Nashville: Thomas Nelson, 1982.

Tournier, Paul.
THE GIFT OF FEELING.
Atlanta: John Knox, 1979

Wagner, Maurice E.
THE SENSATION OF BEING SOMEBODY.
Grand Rapids: Zondervan, 1975.

Wheat, Ed, and Gaye Wheat.
INTENDED FOR PLEASURE.
Old Tappan, N.J.: Revell, 1977.

Wheat, Ed, M.D.
LOVE LIFE FOR EVERY MARRIED COUPLE.
Grand Rapids: Zondervan, 1982.

White, Jerry and Mary.
THE CHRISTIAN IN MIDLIFE.
Colorado Springs: NavPress, 1980.

Wright, H. Norman.
CRISIS COUNSELING.
San Bernardino, Calif.: Here's Life, 1985.

Wright, H. Norman.
COMMUNICATION: KEY TO YOUR MARRIAGE.
Glendale, Calif.: G/L Publications, 1974.

SEASONS OF A MARRIAGE.
Ventura, Calif.: Regal, 1982.

THE CHRISTIAN USE OF EMOTIONAL POWER.
Old Tappan, N.J.: Revell, 1974.

THE HEALING OF FEARS.
Eugene, Ore.: Harvest House, 1982.

Yancy, Philip.
WHERE IS GOD WHEN IT HURTS?
Grand Rapids: Zondervan, 1977

Zunin, Leonard, and Natalie Zunin.
    CONTACT: THE FIRST FOUR MINUTES.
    New York: Ballantine, 1972; Wheaton, Ill.: SP Publica-
    tions, 1973.